BEADING
ACROSS AMERICA
Jewelry Inspirations from Coast to Coast

BEADING
ACROSS AMERICA
Jewelry Inspirations from Coast to Coast

Paulette Baron, Amy Katz, Sherry Serafini

KALMBACH BOOKS

Kalmbach Books
21027 Crossroads Circle
Waukesha, Wisconsin 53186
www.Kalmbach.com/Books

Photography © 2011 Kalmbach Books. Illustrations by Paulette Baron.

Published in 2011
15 14 13 12 11   1 2 3 4 5

Printed in China

ISBN: 978-0-87116-400-1

Publisher's Cataloging-In-Publication Data

Baron, Paulette.   Beading across America : jewelry inspirations from coast to coast / Paulette Baron, Amy Katz, Sherry Serafini.
    p. : ill. ; cm.
    ISBN: 978-0-87116-400-1

    1. Beadwork—United States—Patterns. 2. Beadwork—United States—Handbooks, manuals, etc.
3. Jewelry making—United States—Handbooks, manuals, etc. I. Katz, Amy. II. Serafini, Sherry. III. Title.
TT860 .B37 2011
745.5942/0973

CONTENTS

Midwest

Southwest

Northwest

*Potomac Jewel Earrings
by Amy Katz*

*Three Rivers Rhapsody
Earrings by Sherry Serafini*

The United States is a seed-bead nation filled with bead artistry from coast to coast. Artists come to us from small towns, suburban communities, and metropolitan cities, each contributing their unique style to the craft of beadweaving. While creating art is generally a solitary activity, the collective results become a powerful movement for all to learn from and to admire.

It was our goal to celebrate the talents of the many Americans contributing to the beadstitching world. Drawing from a pool that is as unique as the work itself, we brought together a sampling of some of our country's finest—from long-time, well-known beaders to up-and-coming artists who represent the future of the craft.

Our intention was to assemble a group with very different ideas and points of view. The book is as eclectic as the base of artists in this county. After all, it is the diversity of styles that makes American bead-work great. Some use a cloth-based canvas to create art in embroidery. Others use a loom to plan scenes and designs. Many artists weave beads off-loom. The array of stitches used to create the beadwork gives the book an unrivaled variety. This limitless exploration of creativity is the composition of American bead artistry.

The book explores five regions: the Northeast, the South, the Midwest, the Southwest, and the Northwest. Six artists from different states within each region are featured with their own unique project. Each artist reflects on his or her inspiration and how that translates into beadwork.

A common thread among artists is the influence of environment. As a vast nation, our surroundings are as different as our backgrounds. So how does each unique environment influence the work the artist creates? Travel with us as we explore beading from coast to coast.

You'll find a mix of styles, techniques, and skill levels among the 30 projects presented here. You'll see a summary of techniques and skill levels at the beginning of each project. A stitch tutorial is included to refresh the stitches and other basic skills needed.

American artists create an abundance of seed bead art that is significant nationally and worldwide. *Beading Across America* is our depiction of the American bead dream. Our hope is to both challenge and inspire readers while presenting new ideas and concepts to explore. The pages explode with the talent and pride of our country's artists. We hope you enjoy this book. It truly exemplifies the artistic skills of some of our country's finest beadweavers.

*Dancing Lady
Brooch by
Paulette Baron*

How to use this book

Skill level:
Each project has a designated skill level.

Beginner: Ideal for those new to beadwork.

All levels: Some knowledge of beadwork is required to complete the project.

Intermediate: A good understanding of the stitches is required to complete the project.

Advanced: Proficiency in the stitches is required to complete the project.

Stitch tutorial
The stitch tutorial is a general reference guide to some of the most frequently used stitches and techniques within the book. It's a good place to begin to review stitches and techniques. A conversion chart provides metric equivalents.

Materials lists
Many artists have comfort levels with specific materials. Often readers can get the same results using what best suits their own needs. Below are some variables that should be taken into consideration.

Thread: Many different types of threads are used in this book. Most artists have a specific preference. Choose a thread that works best for you. If you are using crystals and glass pearls, it is best to use FireLine, Wildfire, or other braided threads. For seed-bead based projects, most threads work well.

Conditioning thread: Some artists believe that waxing is essential to the beading process while others never wax a single thread. Choose to wax or not based on what best suits your needs.

Adhesives: The market is filled with different adhesive products. Similar products may be substituted to obtain the same results. Check the products first to make sure they perform the task given in the instructions.

Thread and knots

Conditioning thread

Use either microcrystalline wax, beeswax (not candle wax or paraffin), or Thread Heaven to condition nylon thread. Wax smooths the nylon fibers and adds tackiness that will stiffen your beadwork slightly. Thread Heaven adds a static charge that causes the thread to repel itself, so don't use it with doubled thread. Stretch the thread, then pull it through the conditioner.

Ending thread

To end a thread, weave back into the beadwork, following the existing thread path and tying two or three half-hitch knots (see Half-hitch knot) between beads as you go. Change directions as you weave so the thread crosses itself. Sew through a few beads after the last knot, and trim the thread.

Adding thread

To add a thread, sew into the beadwork several rows prior to the point where the last bead was added. Weave through the beadwork, following the thread path of the stitch. Tie a few half-hitch knots (see Half-hitch knot) between beads, and exit where the last stitch ended.

Stop bead

Use a stop bead to secure beads temporarily when you begin stitching. Choose a bead that is distinctly different from the beads in your project. String the stop bead about 6 in. from the end of your thread, and sew through it in the same direction. If desired, sew through it one more time for added security.

Half-hitch knot

Pass the needle under the thread between two beads. A loop will form as you pull the thread through. Cross back over the thread between the beads, sew through the loop, and pull gently to draw the knot into the beadwork.

Overhand knot

Make a loop with one or more cords. Bring the end of the cord through the loop, and pull tight.

Macramé
Lark's head knot

1. Fold a cord in half, leaving a loop at the top. Bring the loop through the anchor point.
2. Bring the ends of the cord through the loop, and pull until the loop is snugly attached to the anchor point.

Half knot (repeat for spiral)

Spread out the knotting thread keeping the core threads in the middle. The core threads will remain stationary as you work.

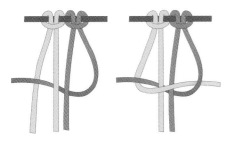

1. Place the right knotting thread under the core and over the left knotting thread.
2. Bring the left thread over the core and down through the loop on the right (made in Step 1). Pull gently on the working ends to tighten.
3. Repeat Steps 1 and 2 until the spiral is the desired length.

Square or flat knot

A square knot is a combination of two half knots, one tied to the right and the other to the left.

1. Follow steps 1–2 of the half-knot instructions to complete the first half of the square knot.

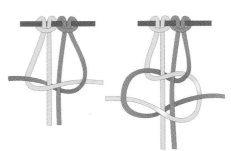

2. Bring the right cord over the core cords and under the left knotting cord. Bring the left knotting cord under the core cords and up through the right loop. Pull gently on the working ends to tighten.
3. Repeat Steps 1 and 2 until the knotted section is the desired length.

Note: To keep track of the side you are working on, notice the working side has the thread facing forward, not back.

Double half-hitch or lark's head sennit

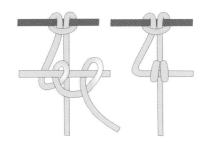

1. Lay one cord across the other cords, and pin it to the macramé board to create a holding cord.

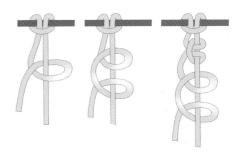

2. Loop the second cord up, over and around the holding cord from back to front, with the tail of the cord pulled to the inside. Tie a second loop exactly the same as the first to complete the knot.
3. Move to the next cord and repeat. Continue tying each cord along the row.

Lei Haku Necklace, by Alethia Donathan, shows macramé.

Stitches

Ladder stitch
Traditional method

1. There are several ways to work a ladder. The most common way is to pick up two beads, sew through the first bead again, and then sew through the second bead (**a–b**).
2. Add subsequent beads by picking up one bead, sewing through the previous bead, and then sewing through the new bead (**b–c**). Continue for the desired length.

While this is the most common technique, it produces uneven tension along the ladder of beads because of the alternating pattern of a single thread bridge on the edge between two beads and a double thread bridge on the opposite edge between the same two beads. You can easily correct the uneven tension by zigzagging back through the beads in the opposite direction. Doing this creates a double thread path along both edges of the ladder. This aligns the beads right next to each other but fills the bead holes with extra thread, which can cause a problem if you are using beads with small holes.

When you're using ladder stitch to create a base for brick stitch, having the holes filled with thread doesn't matter because the rows of brick stitch are worked off the thread bridges, not by sewing through the beads. If you're using the ladder as a base for herringbone stitch, extra thread is potentially problematic, because you'll be sewing through the ladder base more than once.

There are two alternate methods for working ladder stitch, each of which produces beadwork with even tension.

Crossweave method

Center a bead on a length of thread with a needle attached to each end. Pick up a bead with one needle, and cross the other needle through it. Add all subsequent beads in the same manner.

Alternative method

1. To begin the second alternative method, pick up all the beads you need to reach the length your pattern requires. Fold the last two beads so they are parallel, and sew through the second-to-last bead again in the same direction (**a–b**).

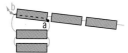

2. Fold the next loose bead so it sits parallel to the previous bead in the ladder, and sew through the loose bead in the same direction (**a–b**). Continue sewing back through each bead until you exit the last bead of the ladder.

If you are working in tubular brick or herringbone stitch, sew your ladder into a ring to provide a base for the new technique. With your thread exiting the last bead in your ladder, sew through the first bead and then back through the last bead, or cross the needles through the first bead if you are using the cross-weave technique.

Brick stitch

1. Work off a stitched ladder (see Ladder stitch). Pick up two beads. Sew under the thread bridge between the second and third beads on the ladder from back to front. Sew up the second bead added and then down the first. Come back up the second bead.

2. For the row's remaining stitches, pick up one bead. Sew under the next thread bridge on the previous row from back to front. Sew back up the new bead.

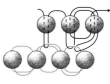

3. To increase at the end of the row, add a second stitch to the final thread bridge in the row.

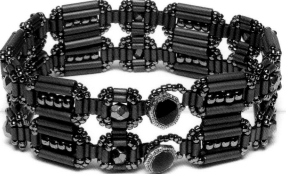

Bugle Blocks Bracelet, by June Huber, uses ladder stitch.

Herringbone

Flat

1. Start with an even number of beads stitched into a ladder (see Ladder stitch). Turn the ladder, if necessary, so your thread exits the end bead pointing up.

2. Pick up two beads, and go down through the next bead on the ladder (**a–b**). Come up through the third bead on the ladder, pick up two beads, and go down through the fourth bead (**b–c**). Repeat across the ladder.

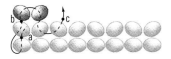

3. To make a turn, sew down through the end bead of the previous row and back through the last bead of the pair you just added (**a–b**). Pick up two beads, sew down through the next bead in the previous row, and sew up through the following bead (**b–c**). Continue adding pairs of beads across the row. You may choose to hide the edge thread by picking up an accent or smaller bead before you sew back through the last bead of the pair you just added.

Tubular

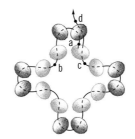

Stitch a ladder (see Ladder stitch) with an even number of beads, and form it into a ring. Your thread should exit the top of a bead.

1. Pick up two beads, and sew through the next bead in the previous round (**a–b**). Sew up through the next bead, and repeat around the ring to complete the round (**b–c**).

2. You will need to step up to start the next round. Sew up through two beads: the next bead in the previous round and the first bead added in the new round (**c–d**).

3. Continue adding two beads per stitch. As you work, snug up the beads to form a tube, and step up at the end of each round until your rope is the desired length.

Herringbone is used throughout An Oregon Bouquet by Virginia Blakelock and Carol Perrenoud.

Peyote

Flat even-count

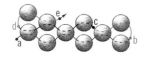

1. Pick up an even number of beads (**a–b**). These beads will shift to form the first two rows.

2. To begin row 3, pick up a bead, skip the last bead strung in the previous step, and sew through the next bead in the opposite direction (**b–c**). For each stitch, pick up a bead, skip a bead in the previous row, and sew through the next bead, exiting the first bead strung (**c–d**). The beads added in this row are higher than the previous rows and are referred to as "up-beads."

3. For each stitch in subsequent rows, pick up a bead, and sew through the next up-bead in the previous row (**d–e**). To count peyote stitch rows, count the total number of beads along both straight edges.

Flat odd-count

Odd-count peyote is the same as even-count peyote, except for the turn on odd-numbered rows, where the last bead of the row can't be attached in the standard way because there is no up-bead to sew through. Work the traditional odd-row turn as follows:

1. Begin as for flat even-count peyote, but pick up an odd number of beads. Work row 3 as in even-count, stopping before adding the last two beads.

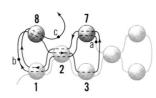

2. Work a figure 8 turn at the end of row 3. Pick up the next-to-last bead (#7), and sew through #2, then #1. Pick up the last bead of the row (#8), and sew through #2, #3, #7, #2, #1, and #8.

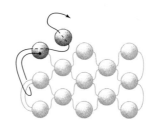

3. You can work this turn at the end of each odd-numbered row, but this edge will be stiffer than the other. Instead, in subsequent odd-numbered rows, pick up the last bead of the row, then sew under the thread bridge immediately below. Sew back through the last bead added to begin the next row.

Tubular

Tubular peyote stitch follows the same stitching pattern as flat peyote, but instead of sewing back and forth, you work in rounds.

1. Start with an even number of beads in a ring.

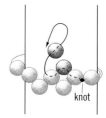

2. Sew through the first bead in the ring. Pick up a bead, skip a bead in the ring, and sew through the next bead. Repeat to complete the round.

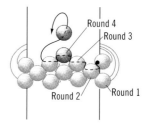

3. You need to step up to be in position for the next round. Sew through the first bead added in round 3. Pick up a bead, and sew through the second bead in round 3. Repeat to achieve the desired length.

New York City bracelet by Suzanne Golden uses tubular peyote.

Decrease

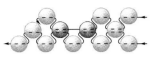

1. At the point of decrease, go through two beads on the previous row.

2. On the next row, when you reach the two-bead space, pick up one bead.

Increase

1. At the increase point, pick up two beads instead of one. Go through the next bead.

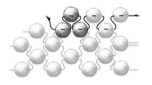

2. When you reach the two beads on the next row, go through the first bead, add a bead, and go through the second bead.

Bezels

The figure shows the pattern for making a bezel around a 16 mm crystal rivoli. The same technique can be used for stones of other shapes and sizes, but you may need to adjust the number of beads picked up in the initial ring as well as the number of rounds stitched, depending on the desired results.

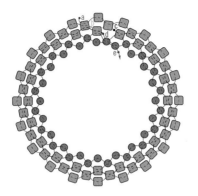

1. Pick up enough 11º cylinder beads (even number) to fit around the circumference of a rivoli or stone, and sew through the first cylinder again to form a ring.
2. Pick up a cylinder, skip the next cylinder in the ring, and sew through the following cylinder. Continue working in tubular even count peyote stitch to complete the round, and step up through the first cylinder added.
3. Work the next two rounds in tubular peyote using 15º seed beads. Keep the tension tight to decrease the size of the ring.

4. Position the rivoli or stone in the bezel cup. Using the tail thread, work one round of tubular peyote along the other edge using cylinder beads, and two rounds using 15ºs.

Zipping up or joining flat peyote

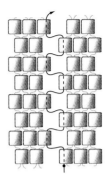

To join two sections of a flat peyote piece invisibly, match up the two pieces so the edge beads fit together. "Zip up" the pieces by zigzagging through the up-beads on both edges.

Laura McCabe's Eiffel Tower Ring has a peyote-stitched bezel.

Right-angle weave (RAW)
Flat

1. To start the first row, pick up four beads, and tie into a ring. Sew through the first three beads again.

2. Pick up three beads. Sew through the last bead of the previous ring (**a–b**) and continue through the first two picked up for this stitch (**b–c**).

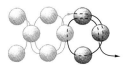

3. Continue adding three beads for each stitch until the first row is the desired length. You are sewing rings in a figure-8 pattern, alternating direction with each stitch.

4. To begin row 2, go through the last three beads of the last stitch on row 1, exiting the bead at the edge of one long side. Pick up three beads, and go back through the bead you exited in the previous step. Continue through the first new bead.

5. Pick up two beads, and go through the next top bead on the previous row and the bead you exited on the previous stitch. Continue through the two new beads and the next top bead of the previous row.

6. Pick up two beads, go through the bead you exited on the previous stitch, the top bead on the previous row, and the first new bead. Keep the thread moving in a figure 8. Pick up two beads per stitch for the rest of the row. When you go back through, don't sew straight lines across stitches.

Tubular

1. To start the first row of right-angle weave, pick up four beads, and tie them into a ring. Sew through the first three beads again.

2. Pick up three beads. Sew through the last bead of the previous ring (**a–b**), and continue through the first two beads picked up in this stitch (**b–c**).

3. Continue adding three beads per stitch until the first row is the desired length. You should be sewing rings in a figure-8 pattern, alternating direction with each stitch.

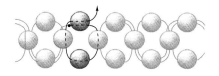

4. Connect the last stitch to the first stitch as follows: Exit the end bead of the last stitch, pick up one bead, sew through the first bead of the first stitch, and pick up one bead. Complete the connecting stitch by retracing the thread path. Exit as shown. In subsequent rounds, you'll add three beads in the first stitch, two beads in the next stitches, and only one bead in the final stitch.

Square stitch

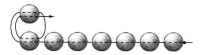

1. String the required number of beads for the first row. Then pick up the first bead of the second row. Go through the last bead of the first row and the first bead of the second row in the same direction as before. The new bead sits on top of the old bead, and the holes are parallel.

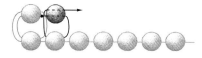

2. Pick up the second bead of row 2, and go through the next-to-last bead of row 1. Continue through the new bead of row 2. Repeat this step for the entire row.

Nevada Flowers and Buds by Susan Barrett demonstrates right-angle weave.

Bead Embroidery

Beaded backstitch
Single bead

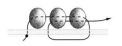

To stitch a line of beads, come up through the fabric from the wrong side. Pick up three beads. Stretch the bead thread along the line where the beads will go, and go through the fabric right after the third bead. Come up through the fabric between the first and second beads, and go through the second and thirds bead again. Pick up three more beads, and repeat. For a tighter stitch, pick up only one or two beads at a time.

Two bead

1. Thread a needle and tie an overhand knot at the end. Sew through the fabric, pick up two beads, and slide flat against the beading material.
2. Sew down through the beading material right below the end of the second bead.
3. Sew back up through the material where you first started, and pass through both beads again.
4. With the needle exiting the second bead, pick up two more beads. Sew down through the material as before.
5. Sew back up through the material between the first and second beads. Sew through the second, third, and fourth beads.
6. Pick up two more beads and continue.

Stop stitch

Sew up through the surface of your beading material. Pick up a larger bead with a flat back or a 6º or 8º seed bead and a smaller seed bead. Skip the small seed bead and pass back through the larger bead and down through the material where you started. This will anchor the larger bead.

Simple edging

1. Secure one end of the thread in your beading material with a few stitches at your starting point along the edge.
2. Sew up through the top edge of the beadwork, pick up a seed bead, and sew back through the foundation to attach.
3. Before tightening the stitch, sew down through the bead. The bead will stand out from the edge of the piece.
4. Pick up another seed bead and continue around the entire piece, sewing through the edges of the material. Once edged the whole way around the work, the last bead will meet the first bead. Go down through the first bead to attach the two. Sew through some beads on the beadwork, making several small knots in the beadwork while hiding them in the beads. Clip the thread close to the beadwork.

Picot edging

Pick up three beads. Measure a distance equal to the size of one seed bead over from the thread and sew down through the edge of the material. Sew back up through the third seed bead and pull snug. Next add two seed beads and sew down through the material, pass the needle back up through the second seed bead strung on. Continue around in this manner.

Wisconsin Memories 1952, by Diane Hyde, uses bead embroidery around the focal piece.

conversion chart

Conversion chart

inch	mm	inch	cm	inch	cm	inch	cm
1/16	2	4¼	10.8	16½	41.9	28¾	73
1/8	3	4½	11.4	16¾	42.5	29	74
3/16	5	4¾	12.1	17	43	29¼	74.3
¼	6	5	13	17¼	43.8	29½	74.9
5/16	8	5¼	13.3	17½	44.5	29¾	75.6
	cm	5½	14	17¾	45.1	30	76
3/8	1	5¾	14.6	18	46	30¼	76.8
7/16	1.1	6	15	18¼	46.4	30½	77.5
½	1.3	6¼	15.9	18½	47	30¾	78.1
9/16	1.4	6½	16.5	18¾	47.6	31	79
5/8	1.6	6¾	17.1	19	48	31¼	79.4
11/16	1.7	7	18	19¼	48.9	31½	80
¾	1.9	7¼	18.4	19½	49.5	31¾	80.6
13/16	2.1	7½	19.1	19¾	50.2	32	81
7/8	2.2	7¾	19.7	20	51	32¼	81.9
15/16	2.4	8	20	20¼	51.4	32½	82.6
1	2.5	8¼	21	20½	52.1	32¾	83.2
1 1/16	2.7	8½	21.6	20¾	52.7	33	84
1⅛	2.9	8¾	22.2	21	53	33¼	84.5
1 3/16	3	9	23	21¼	54	33½	85.1
1¼	3.2	9¼	23.5	21½	54.6	33¾	85.7
1 5/16	3.3	9½	24.1	21¾	55.2	34	86
1⅜	3.5	9¾	24.8	22	56	34¼	87
1 7/16	3.7	10	25	22¼	56.5	34½	87.6
1½	3.8	10¼	26	22½	57.2	34¾	88.3
1 9/16	4	10½	26.7	22¾	57.8	35	89
1⅝	4.1	10¾	27.3	23	58	35¼	89.5
1 11/16	4.3	11	28	23¼	59.1	35½	90.2
1¾	4.4	11¼	28.6	23½	59.7	35¾	90.8
1 13/16	4.6	11½	29.2	23¾	60.3	1 yd.	.9 m
1⅞	4.8	11¾	29.8	24	61	36¼	0.92
1 15/16	4.9	12	30	24¼	61.6	36½	0.93
2	5	12¼	31.1	24½	62.2	36¾	0.93
2⅛	5.4	12½	31.8	24¾	62.9	37	0.94
2¼	5.7	12¾	32.4	25	64	37¼	0.95
2⅜	6	13	33	25¼	64.1	37½	0.95
2½	6.4	13¼	33.7	25½	64.8	37¾	0.96
2⅝	6.7	13½	34.3	25¾	65.4	38	0.97
2¾	7	13¾	34.9	26	66	38¼	0.97
2⅞	7.3	14	36	26¼	66.7	38½	0.98
3	7.6	14¼	36.2	26½	67.3	38¾	0.98
3⅛	7.9	14½	36.8	26¾	67.9	39	0.99
3¼	8.3	14¾	37.5	27	69		m
3⅜	8.6	15	38	27¼	69.2	39⅜	1 m
3½	8.9	15¼	38.7	27½	69.9	1½ yd.	1.4 m
3⅝	9.2	15½	39.4	27¾	70.5	2 yd.	1.8 m
3¾	9.5	15¾	40	28	71	3 yd.	2.7 m
3⅞	9.8	16	41	28¼	71.8	4 yd.	3.7 m
4	10	16¼	41.3	28½	72.4		

Northeast

South

Midwest

Southwest

Northwest

Debra Saucier is a mixed-media artist who has been beading since she was a young girl, and actively teaching since 2006. Debra was named one of the initial CREATE YOUR STYLE with SWAROVSKI ELEMENTS Ambassadors early in 2009 and has taught at the Create Your Style in Tucson Event in 2009, 2010, and 2011. In 2006, Debra and her husband David opened The Bead & Wire Shop. Contact Debra on her websites, debrasaucier.com or beadandwire.com.

Isabelle's Cuff Bracelet

stitches
peyote, netting, wirework
level
advanced

Make the finished bracelet (with frame) ½ in. longer than your wrist size.

supplies
- 11º cylinder beads, **12 g each** of the following colors
    - A: cinnamon gold luster
    - B: apricot topaz gold luster
    - C: sparkling celery lined
- 15º round seed beads, **12 g each** of the following colors
    - D: metallic dark raspberry
    - E: copper-lined alabaster
- **3** 20 x 30 mm oval crystal SWAROVSKI ELEMENTS, fuchsia
- 4 mm SWAROVSKI ELEMENTS bicones, **27 each** of four colors
    - fuchsia
    - chrysolite
    - burgundy
    - crystal copper
- 2 ft. 18-gauge half-hard square sterling silver wire
- 1 ft. 18-gauge half-hard half-round sterling silver wire
- 8 ft. 30-gauge dead-soft round sterling silver wire
- Sonoko Nozue thread
- Size 12 beading needles
- Flatnose pliers
- Chainnose piers
- Nylon jaw pliers
- Painter's tape
- Bracelet mandrel

I've lived in Massachusetts all my life and love that there is always something to stimulate one's mind, soul, and most of all, creativity. Sit and ponder at Thoreau's Walden Pond on a beautiful fall morning or have a lobster bake on the beach at nightfall. Hiking in the dark green mountains or enjoying the beautiful beaches and rocky shorelines are great summer activities. Fall brings spectacular foliage colors, not to mention the wonderful smells from the apple orchards. Winter means snow for skiing and usually ice, which looks like thousands of Swarovski crystals in the early morning sunlight.

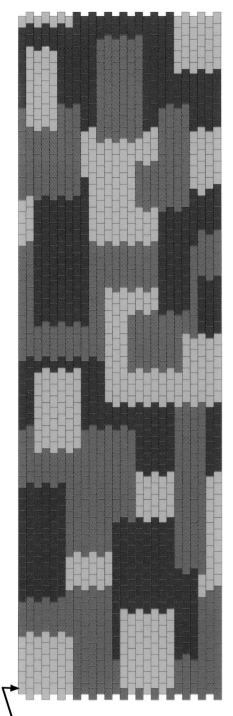

Sparkling
Celery Lined

Apricot Topaz
Gold Luster

Cinnamon
Gold Luster

figure 1

Stitching the peyote band

1. Thread a needle onto a comfortable length of thread. Pick up 26 cylinder beads and follow the pattern to make a flat peyote stitch band 1¼ in. shorter than the desired finished bracelet length (**figure 1**). The wire frame will add length.

Bezeling the stones

2. Thread a needle onto a comfortable length of thread and pick up 68 Ds. Sew through the next bead. Work in peyote stitch around the circle (**figure 2**).

3. Work the next three rows in peyote stitch using As. Keep a tight tension to ensure a proper fit for the oval (**figure 3**).

4. Place a 20 x 30 mm oval crystal front-side down into the peyote bezel. Continue in peyote stitch for two to three more rows using Ds. Tighten the thread every two to three beads. The bezel should start to curve over the back of the oval. Go through the last row of beads again to tighten. Secure the thread in the beadwork (**figure 4**).

Creating the ruffle

5. Thread a needle onto a comfortable length of thread. Secure the thread and position the needle so it exits a cylinder in the middle row. Pick up three Bs and sew through the next cylinder bead in the same row. Repeat until you reach the starting point (**figure 5**).

6. Sew through to the second bead of the new cylinder bead row. Pick up five Bs and sew through the middle of the three beads set on the previous row. Pick up one B, one 4 mm bicone (any color), and one B, and sew through the middle bead of the set of three from the previous row. Repeat until you reach the starting point (**figure 5**).

7. Sew through to the next row of the peyote stitch bezel behind the first ruffle layer. Pick up three Ds, and sew through the next cylinder bead in that row. Repeat until you reach the starting point (**figure 6**).

8. Sew through the starting beads and the two 15ºs from the previous row. Pick up five Es. Sew through the second bead of the next set of three 15º from the previous row. Repeat until you reach the starting point (**figure 6**).

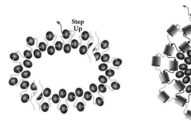

figure 2

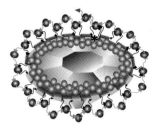

figure 3

figure 4

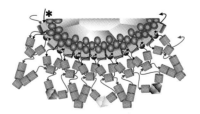

figure 5

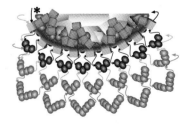

figure 6

9. Sew through to the middle bead of the set of five 15°s from the previous row. Pick up seven Es. Sew through the middle bead of the next group of five 15°s from the previous row. Continue until you reach the starting point (**figure 6**). Tie off the threads between the beads.

10. Repeat Steps 2–9 with the remaining two oval crystals.

Attaching the oval crystals
11. Stitch each oval to the peyote band by sewing it on like a patch. Distribute evenly along the band.

Making the clasp and frame
12. Straighten 2 ft. of square wire using nylon jaw pliers. Use flatnose pliers to create a 90-degree bend in the center of the square wire. Move the pliers just to the side of the bend and create another 90-degree bend (**figure 7**). Repeat on the other side of the center bend to form a diamond shape. Where the wires cross, bend them to become parallel (**figure 8**).

13. Wrap the half-round wire six times around the square wire below the diamond (**figure 8**).

14. Bend the square wires at a 90-degree angle just below the wraps. Make another 90-degree bend about ⅝ in. from the wrap on each wire for a "U" shape (**figure 8**). The peyote band should fit between the wires with 1/16 in. of room on each side.

15. At the other end of the band, bend the wires at a 90-degree angle. The wires will overlap. Create a final 90-degree bend about ¾ in. from the corners. Wrap the wires with a piece of half-round wire and secure with the flatnose pliers. Cut the wire 1 in. from the end of the frame. Use round-nose pliers to bend the end of the wires into a hook (**figure 9**).

16. Cut a 6-in. piece of 30-gauge wire. Working from the back of the peyote band, insert the wire down any one of the outer cylinder beads along the perimeter of the band. Pass the wire up the next cylinder bead, forming a "U" shape out of the wire. The wire will be hidden between the beads.

17. Position the peyote band inside the frame. Wrap one end of the wire several times around the frame. There should only be about a ⅛-in. gap between the peyote band and the wire frame. Pass the wire through a cylinder bead approximately

four beads away. Wrap the wire around the frame again ensuring that the space between the band and the frame is even. Repeat until you have suspended the entire band inside the frame (**figure 10**).

Making the ruffle around the peyote band
18. Thread a needle onto a comfortable length of thread, secure it to the peyote band, and exit an edge cylinder bead. Pick up three Ds. Sew down through the next cylinder bead on the base and up the next one. Repeat around the edge (**figure 11**).

19. Sew through the first cylinder bead of the band and two 15°s from the previous row. Pick up five Bs. Sew through the middle bead of the next group of three 15°s from the previous row. Repeat around the edge (**figure 11**).

20. Sew through the first three cylinder beads from the previous row. Pick up seven Es, and sew through the middle bead of the next group of five cylinders from the previous row. Repeat around the edge. Tie off the thread (**figure 11**).

21. With new thread, sew through the first three cylinder beads from Step 19. Pick up seven Ds and sew through the middle bead of the next group of five cylinders to make another layer of fringe. Pick up two Ds, a 4 mm bicone (any color), and two Ds, and sew through the middle bead of the cylinders. Repeat around the edge (**figure 12**).

22. Using a bracelet mandrel, gently form your bracelet into an oval shape. Use nylon jaw pliers to curve the ends if necessary.

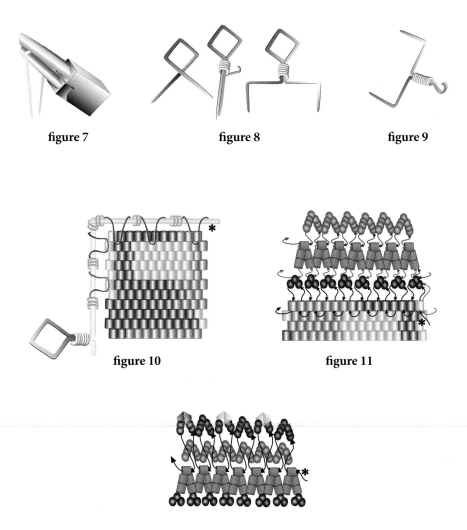

figure 7   figure 8   figure 9

figure 10   figure 11

figure 12

Laura McCabe is a primarily self-taught beadweaver with an education in anthropology and historical costume reproduction and restoration. She produces elaborately beaded body adornment that combines Native American, African Zulu, and Victorian beadweaving techniques with modern materials and color schemes. She exhibits her work in national and international beadwork exhibits, and sells her finished work at boutiques and galleries throughout the United States, as well as through her website, justletmebead.com. She maintains a working studio in Old Mystic, Conn., and teaches beading workshops across the United States and throughout the world.

Eiffel Tower Ring

stitches
herringbone, peyote
level
advanced

supplies
- **6 g** 11º Aikos (must be Aikos)
- **6 g** 11º Delicas (must be Delicas)
- **1 g** 15º seed beads, A (choose a color similar to the Aikos)
- **1 g** 15º seed beads, B (choose a color similar to the Delicas)
- Small amount 15º seed beads, C (color of choice)
- Small amount 15º Japanese charlottes or 13º cuts, D
- **2 g** 15º Czech charlottes, E (D and E are the same color and contrast other beads)
- **2** 5.5 mm pearls
- **14** 3 mm Toho magatama beads
- 48ss crystal point back stone (dentelle, chaton, etc.)
- Size 12 and 13 English beading needles
- FireLine, 6-lb. test
- Microcrystalline wax
- No-tangle bobbin

Despite our reputation as "Old Yankees," I like to think us nutmeggers are beginning to become a little more open minded in the world of jewelry and wearables. I take every opportunity I can to challenge the traditional and conservative style associated with our area by creating jewelry that is modern, edgy, and bordering on avant-garde, while continuing to acknowledge, respect, and maintain the tradition of beadweaving in America. This desire to challenge preconceived notions has inspired much of my work, including this ring with its unique structure and modern yet bold appearance.

Building the bezel base (herringbone)

1. Thread a size 12 needle with 15 ft. of thread. Wax the thread and wind 5 ft. on the bobbin. You will use this tail later to build the stone bezel.

2. Pick up four Aikos and tie a square knot to form a circle of four beads. Sew through the first bead to hide the knot. Pick up two Aikos between each of the four initial beads. Complete the round, and step up (**figure 1**).

3. Pick up two Aikos and work one herringbone stitch. Then pick up one Delica, and go through the next Aiko. Repeat three more times for a total of four herringbone stitches in Aikos with one Delica between each stitch. At the end of the round, step up (**figure 2**).

4. Pick up two Aikos and work one herringbone stitch. Pick up two Delicas, and go through the first Aiko at the top of the next ladder. Repeat three more times, for a total of four herringbone stitches with two Delicas between each stitch. At the end of the round, step up (**figure 3**).

5. Pick up two Aikos and work one herringbone stitch. Pick up one Delica and go through the first of the two Delicas added between the herringbone ladders on the previous row. Pick up two Aikos and go through the second of the Delicas (creating a new herringbone ladder between the two existing ones). Pick up one more Delica before going through the first Aiko at the top of the next ladder. Repeat three more times, for a total of four new herringbone stitches, one between each of the original four. At the end of the round, step up (**figure 4**).

6. Work in herringbone to stitch two Aikos to each of the eight herringbone ladders. Work in peyote to stitch two Delicas between each ladder. At the end of the round, step up (**figure 5**).

7. Work in herringbone to stitch two Aikos to each of the herringbone ladders, and in peyote to stitch three Delicas between each ladder. At the end of the round, step up (**figure 6**).

8. The four newly stitched herringbone ladders (2, 4, 6, 8) will ultimately be the prong points. The longer herringbone ladders (1, 3, 5, 7) will become the base. The beadwork becomes dimensional as the prongs are pushed toward the center.

9. Work in herringbone to stitch two Aikos to the first ladder. Work in peyote to stitch three Delicas and one B between the first and second ladders. Pick up one A between the Aikos on the second ladder. Work in peyote to stitch one B and three Delicas between the second and third ladders. Repeat this process three more times to complete the round. Each of the prong points should have one A. Step up at the end of the round. Wind the working thread onto a bobbin (**figure 7**).

Bezel the stone (peyote)

10. Thread a size 13 needle onto the tail. Sew through the beads to the top of a prong and exit the A at the tip. Pick up 13 beads alternating between Es and As. Finish with an E. Go through the A at the tip of the opposite prong. Pick up 13 more As and Es as before, and sew through the original A tip bead to create a circle (**figure 8**).

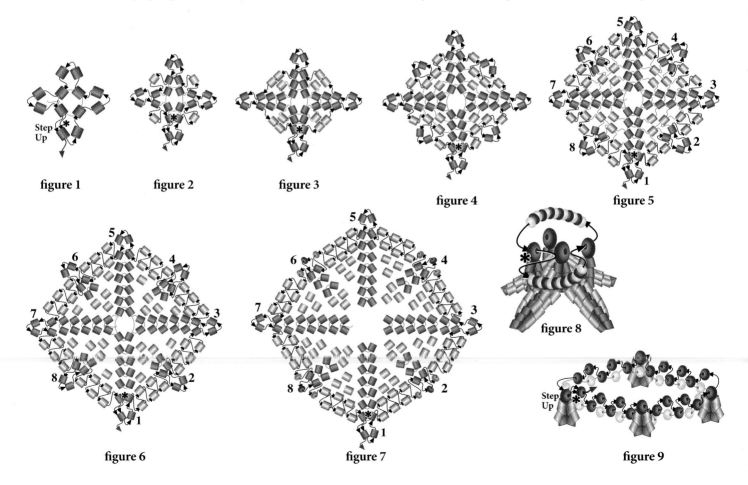

figure 1 figure 2 figure 3 figure 4 figure 5

figure 6 figure 7 figure 8 figure 9

11. Stitch one row of even-count peyote using As between each A on the circle of beads. For the fourth stitch (midway between prongs 1 and 3), use the existing A at the tip on the second prong as the peyote stitch bead, and do not pick up a new bead. Repeat on the other side using the tip of prong 4 as the eleventh A in this peyote stitch row. Remember to step up at the end of the row (**figure 9**).

12. Stitch a row of even-count peyote with Aikos or Delicas (**figure 10**). Then work one row of 3 mm magatamas, and another row of cylinder beads (**figure 11**).

13. Place the stone in the bezel, right side up. Work in peyote to stitch one row of Cs and one row of Es to complete the bezel. Tie half-hitch knots between several beads to secure (**figure 12**).

Embellishing the bezel

14. Once the bezel is complete, embellish the surface. Sew to the top row of cylinder beads. Pick up one D between every bead in the row (**figure 13**).

15. Sew down to the bottom row of cylinder beads. Add a picot of three charlottes between every bead in the row. End the thread by tying half-hitch knots between the beads. Secure and cut (**figure 13**).

Completing the base

16. Thread a size 12 needle onto the bobbin thread. Position the needle so it exits the first of two Aikos in the first herringbone ladder. Pick up one A to finish off the corner, and go down through the second Aiko in this ladder. Pick up three Delicas, four Aikos, and three Delicas. Go up through the first Aiko in the base of the third herringbone ladder (the second corner of the base) (**figure 14**).

17. Stitch one A to the herringbone ladder to finish off the second corner of the base. Peyote stitch two Delicas, and one 5.5 mm pearl. Go down through the second Delica of the next herringbone ladder. Work in peyote to stitch two more Delicas, and exit the first Aiko in the ladder (**figure 14**).

18. Repeat Steps 16–17 for the third and fourth corners of the base. Go through the A and second Aiko at the tip of the first ladder, and sew through the 10-bead base one more time. Go through the first Aiko in the next ladder (at the end of the line of cylinder beads) to begin the peyote ring band (**figure 14**).

Building the band

19. Working off the 10-bead base, stitch a 12-bead-wide band of flat even-count peyote. The first, fifth, sixth, seventh, eighth, and twelfth columns in the band are Aikos. The second, third, fourth, ninth, tenth, and eleventh columns are Delicas (**figure 15**).

20. Stitch the band to the desired length. Zip the last row of the band to the cylinder beads on the other side of the square base.

21. Finish the band by edging it with picots of Czech charlottes on both sides. Tie half-hitch knots between the beads to secure the thread (**figure 16**).

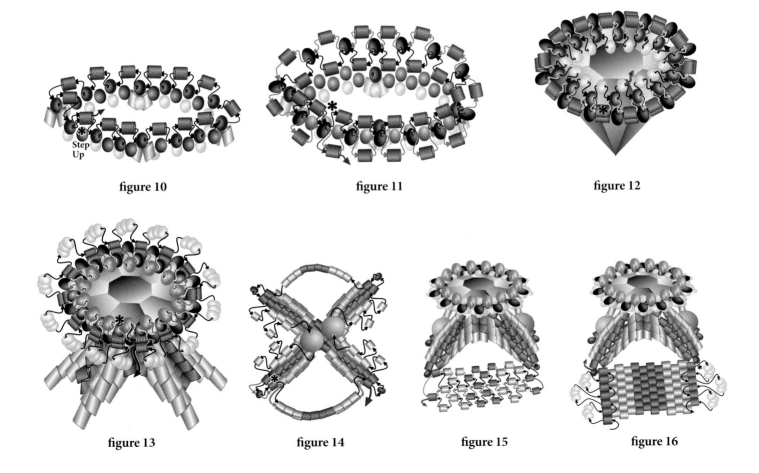

figure 10

figure 11

figure 12

figure 13

figure 14

figure 15

figure 16

Sandy Houk is a perpetual bead hobbyist who enjoys taking classes and learning about the art of beadwork. Inspired by many artists, she found her true love of beads through the works of Diane Fitzgerald and Leslie Frazier. Sandy brings her beadwork everywhere she goes, including motorcycling excursions with her husband where she uses her sidecar as a mini studio.

Spiral Ornament

stitch
netting
level
all levels

supplies
- 11º seed beads, **15 g each** of four colors
    - A: light gold lined
    - B: silver-lined red
    - C: dark gold lined
    - D: silver-lined green
- **24** accent beads, crystals, small holiday decorations, or a mix for the fringe
- Size 12 beading needles
- Nymo D thread
- 2⅝ in. diameter round ornament

New Jersey is a state filled with shapes, colors and lights: my true inspiration. From the suburban streetlights glistening at Christmas time to the beautiful coastal beaches any time of year, there is a lot to see if you open your eyes. Observing this beauty has helped me create bead art. Even more, I delight in sharing my art with my close-knit group of bead buddies who have come to be an important part of my creative life.

Decorating the ornament

Keep the tension tight when stitching the ornament cover.

1. Thread a needle onto 2 yds. of thread. Pick up 11°s in the following order: two As, two Bs, two Cs and two Ds. Repeat the pattern until there are 48 11°s on the thread. Sew through all of the beads again to form a circle. Tie the 11°s tightly into a circle leaving a 6-in. tail. Go through the first A (**figure 1**).
2. Pick up six As and three Bs. Sew through the first B on the ring and down through the three Bs just added (**figure 2**).
3. Pick up three Bs and three Cs. Sew through the first C on the ring. Go back through the three Cs just added (**figure 2**).
4. Pick up three Cs and three Ds. Sew through the first D on the ring. Go back through the three Ds just added (**figure 2**).
5. Continue Steps 3–4 following the corresponding colors, until reaching the

end of the row. For the last stitch of row 1, sew through the next to last D on the ring and go back through the three Ds just added, as before. Pick up three Ds and sew through the first three As (added in Step 2) and the next A on the ring. Go back through five As, exiting through the middle A of the next stitch (**figure 3**).
6. For row 2, pick up six As and three Bs. Sew through the middle B of the previous row and down through the three Bs just added. Continue, picking up three of the color 11°s the needle is exiting and three of the color 11°s the beads will line up with in the previous round (**figure 4**).
7. Repeat Step 6 for one more round.
8. To start row 4, pick up 10 As and five Bs. Repeat Step 6, using five 11°s of each color (**figure 5**).
9. Repeat Step 8 for three more rows using five 11°s of each color (**figure 5**).
10. Put the netting on the ornament as it begins to take form. You may have to adjust the rows depending on the fit (**figure 6**).

11. Repeat Step 8 using three of each 11° instead of five for three rows (**figure 7**).
12. For the next rows, use two of each 11° instead of three (**figure 8**).
13. For the last row, add one corresponding color 11° between every spiral (**figure 9**).

Use smaller or larger beads to change the look. This pattern uses a multiple of eight. To use 15°s start with 64 beads. When using a different size ornament, alter the number of rows.

Creating the fringe

14. Exit a bead on the last row. Pick up 25 11°s of your choice, one accent bead, and three 11°s. Go back through the accent bead and the 11°s. Go through the same bead on the last row (**figure 10**).
15. Sew through to the next bead in the row and repeat. Make 24 fringes.

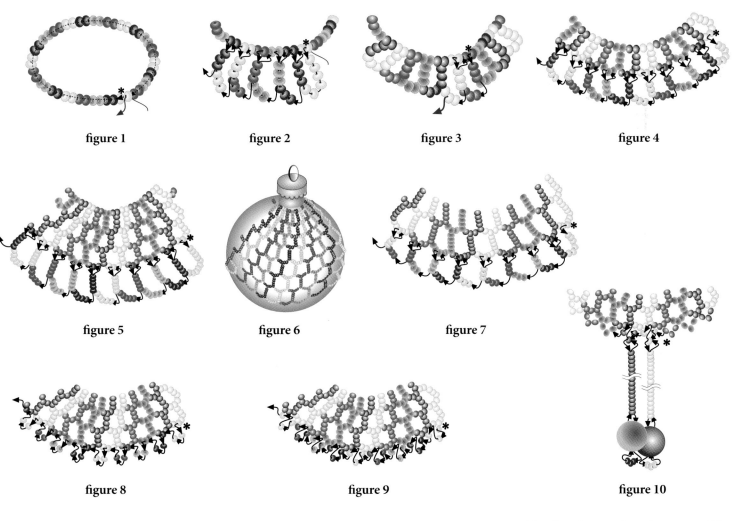

figure 1   figure 2   figure 3   figure 4

figure 5   figure 6   figure 7

figure 8   figure 9   figure 10

Suzanne Golden's work has been featured in juried exhibitions, *Bead&Button* magazine, *Step-by-Step Beads* magazine, and the gallery sections of many books. Her bracelets were featured in *The Art and Elegance of Beadweaving* (Lark 2003), *500 Beaded Objects* (Lark 2004), and most recently two necklaces were included in *500 Plastic Jewelry Designs* (Lark 2009). Contact Suzanne on her website, suzannegolden.com.

New York City Bracelet

Living in New York City is like being wired into a constant source of energy. There is always inspiration to be found in all the different people, stores, and neighborhoods. I wanted my piece to reflect all this activity. The stripes represent the streets and avenues. The flower shape represents Central Park. And in the end, all the different designs come together to form the whole, the same way all the different cultures make up one great city.

stitch
tubular peyote
level
intermediate

supplies
- Czech 6º seed beads, ½ **hank each** of
  black
  white
- Czech 8º seed beads, ½ **hank each** of
  black
  white
- 11º Japanese seed beads, **30 g each** of
  black
  white
- 11º Japanese cylinder beads, **15 g each** of
  black
  white
- 15º seed beads, **15 g each** of
  black
  white
- Power Pro, 15-lb. test or FireLine, 6-lb. test
- Size 12 beading needles
- Pliers
- Thread burner

This bracelet may be made smaller but it is possible that this will cause the design to not line up correctly.

Making the bracelet

1. Thread a needle onto approximately 2 yds. of thread. Put on a stop bead, leaving a 12-in. tail. Follow the chart (**figure 1**) to pick up 48 beads. Sew through all of the beads again to form a circle. Continue through the first two 6º beads.

2. Begin tubular even-count peyote following the pattern. The size of the next bead to pick up is the same size as the bead the thread is exiting (**figure 2**). Step up at the end of the row through both of the 6º beads.

3. Start every row with a 6º and continue to add beads descending in size until reaching the smallest bead in the pattern (15º). Then, still following the pattern, continue to add beads ascending in size until reaching the step up (**figure 3**).

4. Once the bracelet is the length desired, zip the ends of the spirals together.

figure 1

figure 2

figure 3

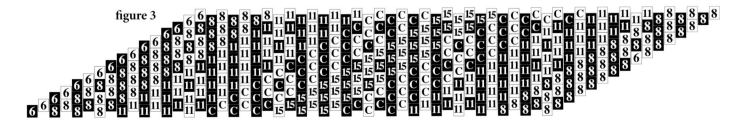

Sherry Serafini is a beadwork artist who has been creating beaded body adornment since 1997. Unusual objects and shapes become part of a new story as she stitches beads and gemstones to a felt-like base. Sherry finds this meditative form of art to be a rich counterpoint to a society full of instant gratification. Sherry lectures and teaches throughout the United States and her work has been published widely. She has won numerous awards for her beaded artwork. She is the author of *Sensational Bead Embroidery* (Lark 2011) and is the co-author of *The Art of Bead Embroidery* (Kalmbach 2007) with Heidi Kummli. Sherry has created beaded adornment for Steven Tyler of Aerosmith, Grammy winner Melissa Etheridge, and several other musicians.

Three Rivers Rhapsody Earrings

Pittsburgh is the home of the Andy Warhol Museum, the Carnegie Museum of Fine Art, and many wonderful centers that support and promote the arts. A stroll through any of these venues can supply endless inspiration, just as a stroll through the Strip District will reveal many art shops, ethnic foods, and street vendors selling their wares. I live half an hour from the inner city and an hour from beautiful mountainous areas. So when the mood strikes for quiet creative time, I head for the hills, and if excitement is on the agenda, a trip downtown is minutes away!

stitches
bead embroidery, peyote, brick
level
all levels

supplies
- **2** 18 mm cabochons
- **2** 10 mm flat round beads
- **2** 6 mm cabochons
- **5 g** cylinder beads, matte finish
- **5 g** 15° seed beads, shiny finish
- SWAROVSKI ELEMENTS
  - **20** 4 mm crystal sequins
  - **14** 3 mm bicone crystals
  - **8** 4 mm round crystals
- 14 in. 14.5ss rhinestone chain, cut into two 3-in. lengths and two 4-in. lengths (rhinestonechain.net)
- **2** 5 x 7 mm or larger crystal drops
- **6** 1½ in. squares Lacy's Stiff Stuff
- **6** 1½ in. squares Ultrasuede in color to match the beads
- Pair of lever-back earring findings
- FireLine, 6-lb. test
- Size 12 beading needles
- E-6000 adhesive
- Wire cutters
- Scissors

Setting up the cabochons
1. Glue the cabochons and the flat round beads each to the center of a Lacy's Stiff Stuff square, and allow to dry.

Making the longer component
2. Thread a needle onto approximately 2 ft. of thread, and knot the end.
3. Begin with the largest cabochon. Sew from underneath the Lacy's, and pick up two cylinder beads. Work in backstitch, bringing the two cylinders down against the Lacy's, and sew down against the second cylinder to the underside of the Lacy's. Come back up through the two cylinders again (**figure 1**).
4. Pick up two more cylinders and sew down against the second cylinder to the underside. Sew up through the last three cylinders added (**figure 2**).
5. Continue in backstitch around the entire cabochon, and end with an even number of cylinders. If there is extra space, pull the thread from the last cylinder added through the first.

6. Using cylinder beads, work even-count peyote stitch over the first row (**figure 3**). Stitch four or five rows of peyote, depending on the depth of the cabochon. Step up at the end of each row. When the cylinder beads begin to get tighter and the spaces are smaller, switch to 15°s to complete the final row (**figure 4**).

Embellishing the large cabochon
7. Sew back to the second row of cylinders from the top, and exit through one of them.
8. Pick up a sequin and a 15°. Sew back through the sequin and the next two or three cylinders in the row. Continue adding sequins around the bezel (**figure 5**).
9. Sew through the underside of the Lacy's, tie off, and cut the excess thread.
10. Carefully trim the Lacy's flush against the beadwork, and glue the cabochon piece to the Ultrasuede. Dry.
11. Trim the Ultrasuede flush against the Lacy's.
12. Using 15°s, work in brick stitch around the cabochon on the edges where the Lacy's and Ultrasuede are glued together (**figure 6**).

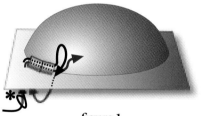

figure 1

figure 2

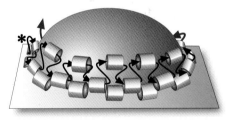

figure 3

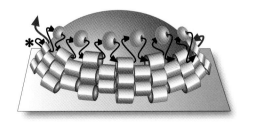

figure 4

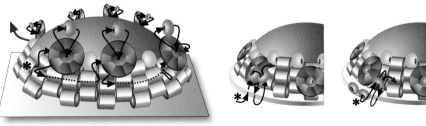

figure 5

figure 6

figure 7

13. Where the last 15º meets the first, sew through one of the edge beads. Pick up four 15ºs, an earring finding, and four 15ºs. Sew through the next 15º edge bead (beside the one previously exited). Go through again to reinforce. Sew through the Lacy's and under the existing beads. Tie off with a small knot, and cut the thread close. Set the two pieces aside (**figure 7**).

Making the middle component

14. Pick up a 10 mm flat bead glued to Lacy's. Wind the rhinestone chain around the bead to see how much length is needed. Use wire cutters to cut the chain.
15. Using a toothpick, spread an even layer of E-6000 around the bead. Gently press the chain into place, allowing small spaces between. Let dry. Work a few small stitches over the top of the chain links for extra security.
16. Repeat Steps 14–15 for the second 10 mm bead unit.
17. Repeat Steps 10–12.

Making the small component

18. Backstitch a row of 15ºs around each 6 mm cabochon. Repeat Steps 10–12.

Attaching the top and middle components (figure 8)

19. Pick up an 18 mm and a 10 mm component. Thread a needle onto about 14 in. of thread, and knot one end.
20. Clip the knot neatly, and bury it between the crystal chains and the Lacy's. Sew through an edge bead.
21. Pick up a 15º, 3 mm bicone crystal, 4 mm round crystal, 3 mm bicone, and a 15º. On the large component, locate the bottom center edge bead opposite the earring finding at the top.

22. Sew up through this edge bead to connect the two components. Sew down through the edge bead beside it.
23. Pick up two 15ºs, 3 mm bicone, 4 mm round, 3 mm bicone, and two 15ºs. Sew down through the edge bead of the middle component next to the first one, creating another attachment.
24. Sew back up through the center attachment and repeat for the attachment on the other side.
25. Sew back through all the attachments to strengthen.

Attaching the bottom component (figure 8)

26. Continue with the working thread. Sew under the chains, and exit the center 15º at the bottom of the middle component.
27. Pick up one 15º, one 4 mm round, and one 15º. Sew through an edge 15º on the small component to attach.
28. Sew up through the 15º on the small component beside the first one exited. Pick up six 15ºs, and go through the corresponding edge 15º on the middle component. Sew back through the 15º, the 4 mm round, and the 15º.
29. Sew over to the 15º on the other side of the center edge bead. Pick up six 15ºs and go through the corresponding 15º on the middle component. Sew through all the attachments again to strengthen them.
30. Sew through the beads and Lacy's. Knot the thread and trim.

Attaching the drop

31. Thread a needle, sew under the small component's beadwork, and locate the center edge bead at the bottom (**figure 8**).
32. Pick up a 15º, 3 mm bicone, seven 15ºs, the drop, and six 15ºs. Sew back up through a 15º, 3 mm bicone, 15º, and the edge bead you started with. Sew through the beads and Lacy's, and knot the thread.
33. Repeat Steps 19–32 to make a second earring to match the first.

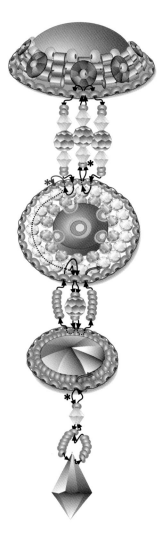

figure 8

Paulette Baron is known for creating three-dimensional sculptural art out of beads. Her pieces use different bead sizes and shapes and a wide assortment of off-loom beadweaving stitches. She teaches classes at several national bead shows. Paulette's *Pinwheel Garden* necklace appears on the title page of Margie Deeb's book, *The Beader's Color Palette* (Watson-Guptill 2008). Her work is featured in *Beading with Brick Stitch* (Interweave 2001) by Diane Fitzgerald, *The Art of Beadweaving Stitches: The Best Collection of Beadweaving Stitches by 9 American Bead Artists* by Kumiko Mizuno Ito, in the Bead Dreams Exhibit, and in *The Beaded Figure* traveling exhibition. Visit her website, paulettebaron.com.

Dancing Lady Brooch

Being an artist by trade and at heart, any kind of art has always been my true inspiration. Living in culturally rich Maryland, I have a wealth of resources to ignite this passion. Maryland and its surrounding states are brimming with artistic treasures—from close-by museums in Washington, D.C., to once-in-a-lifetime exhibits like the work of Joyce Scott presented in Baltimore not long ago. This state has helped me live and breath the art I love as I express myself through the medium of beads.

stitch
brick
level
intermediate

supplies
- 8º seed beads, **1.5 g each** of four colors
  A: purple
  B: aqua-lined fuchsia
  C: light purple AB
  D: dark raspberry AB
- 8º hex beads **1 g** E: dark purple AB
- 8º triangle beads **2 g** F: raspberry-lined AB
- 11º seed beads, **1.5 g each** of six colors
  G: purple
  H: aqua-lined fuchsia
  I: light purple AB
  J: raspberry-lined AB
  K: dark raspberry AB
  L: transparent purple
- 11º triangle beads **1 g** M: metallic purple AB iris
- 10º twisted hex beads **1 g** N: transparent purple
- 15º **1 g** silver-lined AB
- 12 x 8 mm (approx.) oval bead
- **2** 3 x 11 mm top-drilled daggers
- **2** 3 x 5 mm top-drilled drops
- Pinback
- Nymo D thread
- Size 12 beading needles
- Beading wax

Creating the body

1. Center a needle onto 3 yds. of thread, and wax the thread doubled.
2. Work brick stitch to make a 5 x 5 bead square (bead ladder row plus two-drop rows) with As (**figure 1**).
3. Fold the square so that column four is on top of column three. Sew down through column four, and go up through the bottom three As of column one. Attach the columns only between these beads. Reinforce by sewing down through two As in column two and the bottom A in column one. Attach again through the bottom A in column four. The bead square will fan out to form a "V" (**figure 2**).
4. Sew up through two more beads in column four and over and through the top two beads in column five (**figure 2**).

Creating the skirt and leg

5. Start a new bead ladder off the square as shown, picking up five Es, five Bs, five Fs, and five Cs. Reinforce the last two Cs by looping through them again. The needle should exit the top of the last C in the ladder.

6. Work in brick stitch back towards the square using smaller beads in similar colors to those on the bead ladder row (Color I over C, J over F, H over B, M over E). Start each new row with an increase by picking up two beads and going under the first thread loop (**figure 3**).
7. If the bead on the top doesn't cover most of the hole of the bead below, increase by adding the same size bead to the same loop thread. The more beads added in each row, the more the beadwork will ruffle and curl. End each row with an increase, by adding a second bead onto the last loop of thread. Begin the next row with an increase.
8. Stitch three full rows and three quarters of the fourth row to form the skirt and legs. Gradually shift the colors of the beads to avoid sharp vertical lines between the colors (**figure 4**).
9. Lay the square with the bead ladder to the left, folded side down. Sew to the last F on the bead ladder row. Fold the skirt over and connect the F to the A on the bottom right of column one. Reinforce the connection between the two beads (**figure 4**).

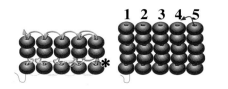

figure 1

figure 2

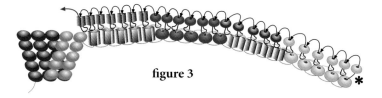

figure 3

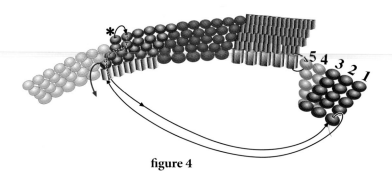

figure 4

10. Manipulate, fold, and curl the bead ladder row to form the skirt and stitch it in place. To keep the skirt in the desired shape, connect a bead from the bead ladder to a bead on the square. Reinforce in several places. Beads E and M, B and H, and F and J become the skirt. Beads C and I become the legs.

Adding the feet

11. Exit through the last I on the leg. Pick up one 15º, a top-drilled dagger, and three 15º s. Sew up through the next bead of the leg. Pick up three 15º s, a top-drilled dagger and five 15º s. Sew through the next two leg beads. Knot the thread and trim (**figure 5**).

Creating the upper body

12. Thread a needle, and start a new bead ladder from the end bead at the top of the square to form the shoulders, arms and upper body. Begin with five Ks and five 15º s (**figure 5**).

13. Exit through the top bead of the ladder. Brick stitch back towards the square, increasing at the start as before, using the same size and color as the ladder.

14. Continue across the top of the square with Ds, with a decrease.

15. Begin the next row with a decrease, using Ks across the square and a few beads over the 11º s of the arm.

16. The next row will start and end with decreases. The top row will have three Ks (**figure 5**).

Creating the head and hair

17. Pick up one C for the neck, the oval bead, one A, and eight Gs for kinky fringe. Skip the last bead and sew down through three Gs. Add four more Gs, skip the last bead, and go through the Gs, the A, the oval, the C and one K of the top row of the shoulder. Sew through five more shoulder beads and exit another K on the top row (**figure 6**).

18. Go back up through the C, the oval, and the A and make another kinky fringe with another color of 11º s. Repeat several times to secure the oval bead, going through each of the three Ks at the top of the shoulder (**figure 6**).

19. Once the oval (head) bead does not flop over, continue to add kinky fringe

hairs and loops with some coming only under the A at the top of the head (**figure 6**).

Creating the finishing touches

20. Add another arm if desired on the opposite side of the square, following Steps 12–14.

21. Exit the first D in the row above the square closest to the arm. Pick up a top-drilled drop and go through the next D of this row. Sew around to come back out of the same D. Add the other top-drilled drop through the following D (**figure 6**).

22. To make the skirt fuller, stitch a small bead ladder attaching the body to the skirt. Exit the last K on the upper body and add five Ds and five Ns. Attach the ladder to the 11º in the second row of the skirt. Continue adding rows of Ls (over Ns) and Ks (over Ds) until you reach the desired fullness (**figure 7**).

23. Sew a pinback onto the back of the bead square or use one of the hair loops as a bail for a pendant.

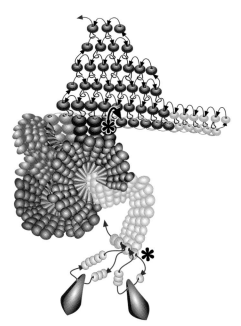

figure 5

figure 6

figure 7

Amy Katz has been part of the world of seed beads since 1993 as a student, teacher, and designer. High-end jewelry has always been something she has admired and loved. Several years ago when she began designing her own beadwork pieces, Amy decided to create a fine-jewelry look with seed beads and crystals. Using imagination and top-notch materials, this vision has materialized into her signature style. Amy teaches nationally. Visit beadjourney.com to see more of Amy's work.

Photo: Esta R. Gladstone

Potomac Jewel Earrings

stitches
peyote, right-angle weave
level
intermediate

supplies
- **1.5 g** 11º cylinder beads, silver
- **.5 g** 15º round seed beads, silver
- **.6 g** 15º charlottes, silver
- SWAROVSKI ELEMENTS pearls
    2 10 mm white
    2 8 mm white
    14 3 mm white
- **54** 2 mm SWAROVSKI ELEMENTS round crystals, crystal AB
- FireLine, 6-lb. test
- Pair of earring wires
- Size 12 beading needles

I enjoy watching northern Virginians as they hustle about trying to grab the proverbial brass ring. Many have done so, as elegant homes line many streets, and every type of shopping experience can be found here. All of this exists among the beautiful colors that nature provides in spring and fall; a display that brings a magical touch to the atmosphere. I too wanted to create my own sense of elegance and excitement. As a result, I have made my accomplishment my bead art and my brass ring the fine-jewelry style I have come to call my own.

Stitching the top cap

1. Thread a needle onto 2½ yds. of Fire-Line, and pick up one 8 mm pearl. Leave a 12-in. tail.

2. Pick up eight cylinder beads. Go through the pearl and through the cylinder beads again, creating a semicircle on one side of the pearl (**figure 1**).

3. Go up through the pearl again. Repeat Step 2 on the other side of the pearl, creating a second semicircle (**figure 1**).

4. With the needle exiting the eighth cylinder bead, pick up two cylinder beads. Go back through the first semicircle. Pick up two more cylinder beads, and go back through the second semicircle and one of the two beads just added. There should be 20 cylinder beads around the pearl (**figure 2**).

5. Work five rows of peyote stitch around the circle with cylinder beads. Make sure to step up at the end of each row (**figure 3**).

6. Work one row of peyote stitch with charlottes. Thread a needle onto the tail, and stitch another row of peyote with charlottes on the opposite end of the pearl cap (**figure 4**).

7. Choose a front and back side of the cap. On the front side, sew through to the first row of ditches. Stitch-in-the-ditch all the way around with 2 mm round crystals (**figure 5**).

8. Leave all threads in place.

Making the connector

9. Thread a needle onto the longer thread remaining from Step 8, and sew through to the middle of the peyote section. Go through two cylinder beads.

10. Pick up six 15°s. Using the cylinder-bead base as the start, stitch the first right-angle weave (RAW) square (consisting of two cylinder beads and six 15°s) (**figure 6**).

11. Stitch four more squares of RAW, picking up six 15°s each time. Leave the needle in place (**figure 6**).

Stitching the bottom cap

12. Follow Steps 1–4 with these variations: Pick up a 10 mm pearl, and use 10 cylinder beads for each semicircle. There will be 24 cylinder beads around the 10 mm pearl.

13. Stitch six rows of peyote with cylinder beads.

14. Repeat Step 6.

15. Choose the front and back of the

earring. On the front, position the needle on the top row of ditches. Stitch-in-the-ditch with one 2 mm crystal. Move to the next ditch. Pick up a 3 mm pearl and a 2 mm crystal. Go back through the 3 mm pearl and the next ditch. Continue alternating all the way around, adding 2 mm crystals and 3 mm pearls. End the threads by tying half-hitch knots between the beads (**figure 7**).

Decorating the right-angle weave connector

16. Pick up the connector. Thread a needle onto the existing thread and stitch one more square of RAW. Pick up two 15°s, and go through two cylinder beads in the middle on the second cap. Pick up two 15°s, and go through all eight beads of this square again to reinforce the connection (**figure 8**).

17. Sew through to the top beads of the next square. Pick up a 3 mm pearl, and sew it between the next square of RAW, with the thread exiting in the opposite direction on the opposite side of the square.

18. Pick up a 2 mm crystal between the two 15°s on both the right and left sides of the next RAW loop. Sew through to the top of the loop (**figure 9**).

19. Repeat steps 17 and 18.

20. Sew through the beadwork into the top cap. End the thread by tying half-hitch knots between the beads.

Adding the finding

21. Using the remaining thread, come out of the center on top of the cap, pick up three cylinder beads, one earring finding, and three cylinder beads. Sew the thread into the next ditch. Reinforce by sewing through the beads and finding again. Sew through the beadwork to secure the thread (**figure 9**).

22. Make a second earring to match the first.

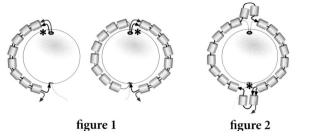

figure 1   figure 2

figure 3

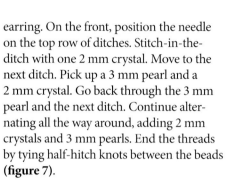

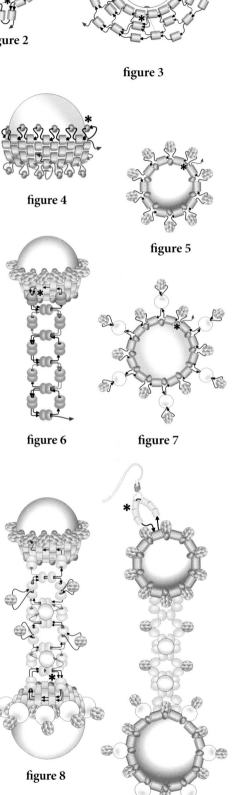

figure 4

figure 5

figure 6   figure 7

figure 8

figure 9

Carol Wilcox Wells is an artist, teacher, and author. Her two books, *Creative Bead Weaving* (Lark 1996) and *The Art & Elegance of Beadweaving* (Lark 2002), are among top-selling bead titles. Carol also has compiled two other books, *500 Beaded Objects: New Dimensions in Contemporary Beadwork* (Lark 2004), and *Masters Beadweaving: Major Works by Leading Artists* (Lark 2008). Her work has been collected and exhibited internationally and featured in publications including: *Ornament, Lapidary Journal, Bead&Button, Beadwork* and several books. She teaches basic and advanced beadweaving to hundreds of students in the U. S. and in England. Carol lives in Hot Springs, N.C., where she is currently pursuing her creative spirit. Visit schoolofbeadwork.com.

Sunset Bracelet

There is nothing that compares with the beauty of the mountains of western North Carolina, at least for me. This place is in my soul and speaks to me like no other. I live in a very rural area where wildlife and nature abound. Rabbit, turkey, bobcat, coyote, and black bear are my neighbors (and maybe a couple of humans, too). Each day is a delight, as I come across a wild flower or interesting fungus. Each evening the sky fills with wonder: a bounty of color and visual emotion. Truly a creative person's dream come true.

stitches
chevron chain, right-angle weave, peyote, herringbone
level
intermediate

supplies
- 11º seed beads, **5 g each** of three colors
    A: color-lined orange sherbet
    B: color-lined yellow
    C: color-lined turquoise
- 15º seed beads, **5 g each** of two colors
    D: silver-lined light green
    E: silver-lined orange AB
- SWAROVSKI ELEMENTS
    14 mm rivoli, fuchsia
    4 4 mm rose montees, Topaz
    10 SS39 Caribbean blue opal chatons #1028
- Nymo D thread: orange, light green, turquoise
- Size 12 and 13 beading needles
- **4** jumbo metal paper clips or 16- or 18-gauge wire
- Wire cutters

Making the bracelet base using chevron chain

1. Thread a needle onto 5 ft. of orange thread. Pick up a stop bead and leave a 6-in. tail.

2. Pick up 12 beads in the following order: five As, three Bs, and four As. Sew back through the first bead to form a triangle (**figure 1**).

3. Pick up seven As and sew through bead 9 of Stitch 1 (**figure 2**).

4. Pick up three Bs and four As. Stitch up through bead 4 of Stitch 2 (**figure 2**).

5. Repeat Stitches 2 and 3 until there are a total of 55 stitches. End the working thread and the tail using knots in the A beads only.

6. Repeat Steps 1–5 to make a second chevron chain strip.

Connecting the bracelet base with two-needle right-angle weave

7. Lay the two chevron chain strips on a flat surface with the Bs on the inside edge.

8. Thread a needle onto each end of a 5-ft. piece of orange thread. Use one of the needles to pick up three Bs. Sew through the first group of three Bs on the left. With the other needle, sew through the first group of three Bs on the right. Center the thread so that equal amounts are on each side (**figure 3**).

9. Pick up three Bs with the right needle and sew through three Bs on the left side. Pick up one D and sew through three Bs of Stitch 5 on the left (**figure 3**).

10. With the left needle, sew through beads 1, 2, 3, and three Bs on the right side. Pick up one D and sew through three Bs of Stitch 5 on the right (**figure 3**).

11. Continue adding crossbars of three Bs between Stitches 7–49 (23 more crossbars). Make the larger opening between Stitches 52–53. Reinforce the two large openings a few times.

Making the star bezels with peyote and herringbone

12. Thread a needle onto 4 ft. of light green thread. Sew through two A beads between Stitches 2 and 3. Make a knot, and continue through the next three A beads and one B bead of Stitch 1 (**figure 4**).

13. Row 1: Pick up one D, skip the next B, and sew through the following bead. Continue around using peyote until there are six stitches. Step up at the end of the row (**figure 4**).

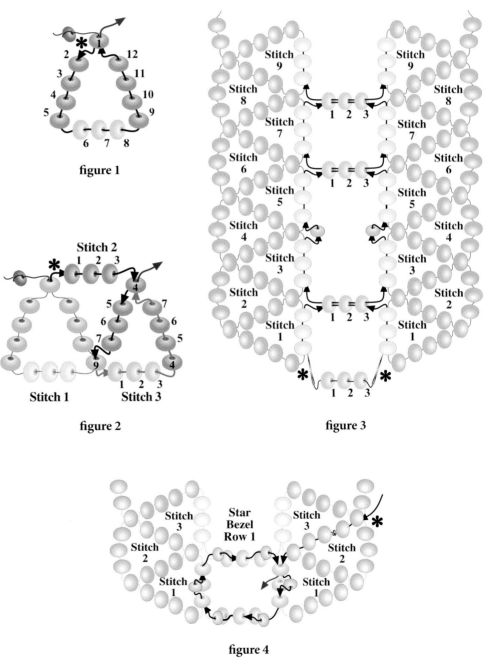

figure 1

figure 2

Stitch 1   Stitch 3

figure 3

figure 4

14. Row 2: Work another row of peyote stitch with Ds. Step up at the end of the row (**figure 5**).

15. Row 3: Work a row of two-drop peyote stitch with Ds. Step up at the end of the row through two Ds (**figure 6**).

16. Row 4: Work another row of two-drop peyote. At the step up, go through three Ds instead of four to split the first group in this row (**figure 7**).

17. Row 5: To work one row of herringbone, pick up two color Ds, sew through the next 15º on Row 4, and the two 15ºs on Row 3. Exit through the next 15º on Row 4. Repeat, making a total of six herringbone stitches. Exit through the first bead added in this row (**figure 8**).

18. Row 6: Work one row of herringbone using three Ds in each stitch to form a picot, and pick up two Ds between each

herringbone picot stitch. End the row with the needle exiting the first 15º of the pair added between herringbone stitches (**figure 9**).

19. Row 7: Stitch a three-bead picot row using Ds, splitting the two 15ºs added between the herringbone stitches of the previous row. Follow the thread path in Figure 8. End with the needle exiting the middle 15º of the first picot in this row (**figure 10**).

20. Row 8: Sew through the point of each picot in Row 7, picking up two Ds between each point (don't tighten the thread). Place a chaton into the center of the bezel and the circle of beads. Now, tighten the beads around the crystal. Reinforce it several times and end the thread (**figure 11**).

21. Follow Steps 12–19 to stitch the remaining star bezels (10 in total).

To make the point of each star intersect with a valley of the next star, alternate where the first row of peyote begins by one bead. For example, the first star began its peyote row from bead one. Start the second star from bead two. Then start the third from bead one again.

Making the sun bezel

22. Thread a needle onto 5 ft. of thread. Pick up 24 Es. Tie the beads into a circle.

23. Follow Steps 13–19, using Es. For Row 8, pick up only one 15º between each picot point. Place the rivoli in the center and sew through all the beads in the circle several times. Sew through to the back of the bezel, and exit one of the beads in Row 1.

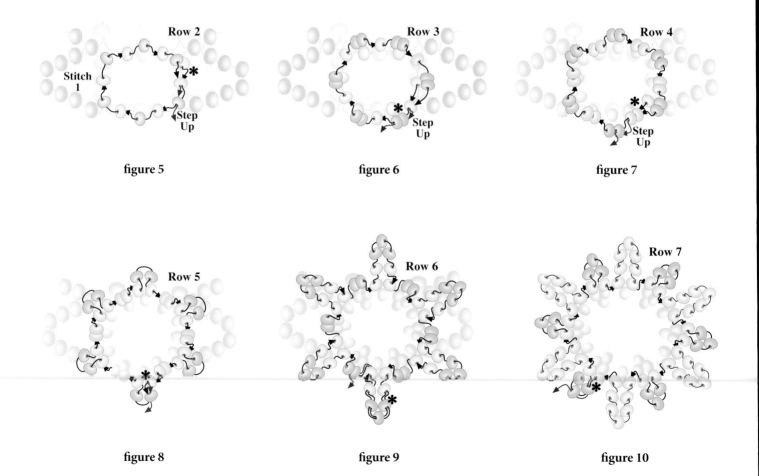

figure 5

figure 6

figure 7

figure 8

figure 9

figure 10

Making the peyote strip (on the back of the sun bezel)

24. Use Es and work two peyote stitches.
25. Turn and stitch a flat peyote strip four beads wide by 14 rows long, counting on the diagonal (**figure 12**).
26. Attach the peyote strip to the opposite side of the Sun Bezel in Row 1. It will be very tight. Reinforce and end the thread.

Making the toggle

27. Thread a needle onto 4 ft. of turquoise thread. Pick up a stop bead, and leave a 6-in. tail.
28. Pick up 19 Cs and work back in peyote. Continue with odd-count peyote stitch for 12 rows. Remove the stop bead, secure the tail in the beadwork and knot. Cut the excess thread.
29. Roll the tube lengthwise, and zip the edges together. Make sure to join the last bead (**figure 13**).
30. Using the working thread, sew a rose montee on the end of the tube. Sew through to the opposite end (**figure 14**).
31. Open one of the metal paper clips, and cut it into three pieces the length of the tube (or substitute 16–18 gauge wire) to fit snugly inside the tube (**figure 14**).
32. Sew another rose montee on this end of the tube, and sew through to bead 9 in the center of the tube.
33. Make another toggle, following Steps 27–32.
34. Using Cs, make a three-bead-wide peyote stitch strip. Pick up one bead and stitch into bead 11. Turn, pick up another bead, and stitch through the first new bead and bead 9. Turn, then pick up a bead, and sew through the first new bead and bead 11. Turn, and sew through the second new bead added (**figure 15**).
35. Continue stitching until there are 20 beads along the outside edge. To lengthen the bracelet, make this peyote strip longer.
36. Center the sun bezel on the three-bead-wide peyote strip.
37. Attach this strip to the center of the second toggle, and reinforce.
38. To attach the clasp, slide the sun bezel to one end, and put the toggle through the large opening in the bracelet base. Slide the sun bezel towards the star bezel, place the bracelet on your wrist, and pull the second toggle through the large opening on the other side of the base. Slide the sun bezel so it is centered between the ends of the bracelet.

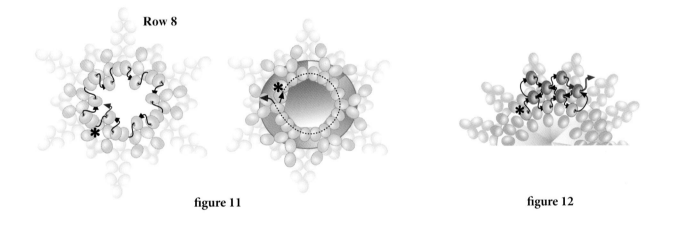

Row 8

figure 11

figure 12

figure 13

figure 14

figure 15

Sandy Martin started beading in 2002 when she bought a new sewing machine and, in the same shop, discovered the beaded creations of her friend and mentor, Diane Cagnon Ciolek. Sandy has always been involved in some type of needlework, but she quickly developed a passion for seed beads. Now a retired partner from a large consulting firm, Sandy spends many of her days traveling, looking at all the beauty in the world, and thinking about ways to translate that beauty into beading.

Appalachian Mist Bracelet

The Commonwealth of Kentucky is a beautiful and varied place. From the mountains in the east, past the rolling bluegrass and horse farms, through large cities and small towns, along major rivers, to the lake country of the west, the scenery is always changing and always intriguing. We have four full seasons with all of the colors and changes that come with them. I especially love the mountains and the mist that appears around them very early in the morning when it's still almost dark. That's when my heart feels most at peace. This square-stitch bracelet uses a simple blending technique to blend from dark blue to olivine and back to blue again, depicting the mist in and around the mountains of Kentucky.

Making the bracelet base

1. Thread a needle onto a comfortable length of thread, and wax thoroughly. Attach a stop bead, leaving a 6-in. tail.

Each color-blended section consists of 15 rows, 13 rows with blended beads and two solid rows. Each section is 1³⁄₁₆ in. long. The bracelet ends should be about ½ in. from each other when wrapped around the wrist. If an additional full section makes the bracelet too long, increase the number of solid color rows at the start, the end, or between each blended section.

2. Pick up 14 As. Work one row of square stitch with As **(figure 1)**.
3. In Row 3, begin the blending technique using one B and 13 As. Add the B anywhere in the row.
4. Follow the pattern **(figure 2)** through Row 15, adding one B and reducing one A in each new row.

5. Rows 16 and 17: Use all Bs **(figure 3)**.
6. Row 18: Reverse the process. Start with one A and 13 Bs. Continue adding one more A and reducing one B in each row through Row 30.
7. Rows 31 and 32: Use all As.
8. Repeat Rows 1–32 five times or to desired length.

Blending Tips: Don't avoid using the new color on the edges of the bracelet. Once half of the new color is added in a row, think of it as reducing the original and adding the new color.

Embellishing the edges

9. Thread a needle onto a comfortable length of thread, and wax. Determine which is the top and bottom of the bracelet. Start the edge at the same point on both sides of the bracelet. Decide which is the front side and position the needle so that it exits the edge bead of Row 1.

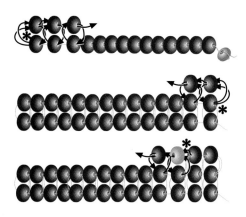

figure 1

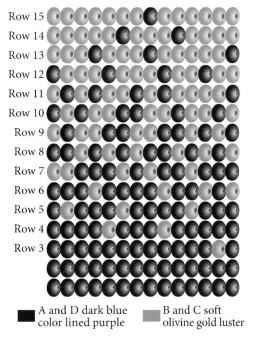

■ A and D dark blue color lined purple
■ B and C soft olivine gold luster

figure 2

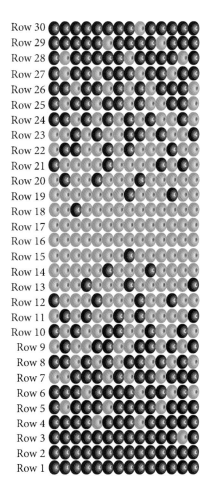

figure 3

10. Pick up two Cs, one crystal, and two Cs. Skip edge bead 2 and sew into edge bead 3 (**figure 4**).

11. Sew back through edge bead 2, exiting in front of the beads just added (**figure 4**).

12. Pick up seven Cs and sew into edge bead 4 (**figure 5**).

13. Sew back through edge bead 3, exiting in front of the beads just added (**figure 5**).

14. Repeat Steps 8–11 across the length of the bracelet. Weave in the thread, tie off and end (**figure 6**). Repeat Steps 9–14 on the opposite side.

Attaching the clasp

15. Thread a needle onto a comfortable length of thread. Secure the thread in the beadwork, exiting the fourth bead of Row 1 (**figure 7**).

16. Pick up six Ds, go through one clasp loop and sew through beads 5 and 6, and exit bead 7.

17. Pick up six Ds, go through the next clasp loop and into beads 8 and 9, and exit bead 10. Pick up six more Ds, go the last loop of the clasp and beads 11 and 12. Weave in the thread, tie off and end.

18. Repeat Steps 15–18 on the other end to attach the other clasp half.

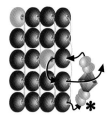

figure 4

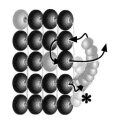

figure 5

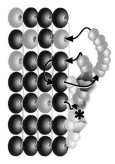

figure 6

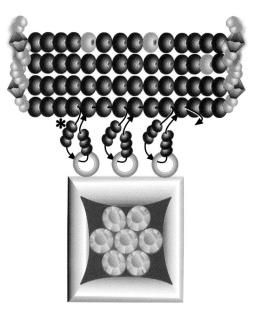

figure 7

Margie Deeb brings an unstoppable passion for creativity and beauty to everything she does. She is the author of *The Beader's Guide to Color* (Watson-Guptill 2004) and *The Beader's Color Palette* (Watson-Guptill 2008). Her work is displayed across the U.S. in galleries and boutiques. Margie has taught collegiate color and design, she has been a guest instructor at the Sonoma Beadwork Retreat, she teaches at BeadFest, and has taught at the Bead Museum in Arizona and bead stores and societies across the country. Margie writes regularly for *Bead&Button* and *Beadwork* magazines, and her work has appeared in numerous books and calendars. She publishes a free monthly color column and podcast on her website, margiedeeb.com.

Colorful Coin Collar

I love to wear and create bold jewelry—jewelry with a presence that commands attention and makes a statement. Broadcollars are a prime example of this. The Egyptian collection at the Carlos Museum at Emory in Atlanta keeps me inspired. They have some of the oldest known Egyptian jewelry and broadcollars. As for color, Georgia's palettes in the spring and fall are exceptionally luminous. I'm moved by the brilliance and clarity of our colors (when temperatures aren't too high).

stitch
right-angle weave, fringe
level
all levels
supplies
- **5 g** 11º seed beads, 24K gold plated
- 6.5 mm coin beads
   - **57** cobalt (6.5 C)
   - **54** vitrail (6.5 V)
   - **32** light cobalt (6.5 LC)
- 10 mm coin beads
   - **17** cobalt AB (10 CA)
   - **15** light cobalt (10 LC)
- 14.5 mm coin beads
   - **11** cobalt (14.5 C)
   - **5** vitrail (14.5 V)
- Centerpiece focal bead or button (approx. 35 mm)
- Two-strand clasp
- Nymo D thread
- Size 10 beading needles
- Pins (optional)
- ¼-in. thick sheet foamcore
- Glue

Making the foundation row

1. Make an armature disc out of foamcore to ensure the necklace has a natural curve. Measure a 5⅛-in. diameter circle on the foamcore, and cut it out. Glue the disc to a 10½ x 10½ in. foamcore base, 2 in. from the top.

2. Thread a needle onto 5 ft. of thread, and pick up a stop bead, leaving a 5 in. tail.

3. Pick up one 6.5 mm vitrail coin (6.5 V), one 11º seed bead, one 6.5 cobalt coin (6.5 C), one 11º, one 6.5V , one 11º, one 6.5 light cobalt coin (6.5 LC), and one 11º. Sew through the first five beads again and exit the second vitrail coin (**figure 1**).

4. Pick up one 11º, one 6.5 LC, one 11º, one 6.5 V, one 11º, one 6.5 C, and one 11º. Sew through the V the thread is exiting, the 11º, the LC, and the 11º, and exit the last vitrail coin (**figure 2**).

5. Pick up one 11º, one 6.5 C, one 11º, one 6.5 V, one 11º, one 6.5 LC, and one 11º. Sew through the V the thread is exiting, the 11º, the C, the 11º, and exit the last vitrail coin (**figure 2**).

6. Repeat Steps 4 and 5, keeping the foundation flat and working around the foamcore armature disc. Use gentle tension to make the foundation curve around the disc. To make a 16 in. necklace, use 33 vitrail coins, plus the clasp. To make a different length, make sure there are an odd number of vitrail coins (**figure 3**).

7. Sew back through the squares in a circular pattern, and tie off. Snip both the tail and the working thread.

Stringing the fringe

8. Thread a needle onto 3 ft. of thread, and secure it at one end of the foundation row. Snip the tail. Make 25 fringes. The longest center fringe (#13) will hang directly beneath the center 6.5 mm vitrail coin.

9. Count 12 vitrail coins from the center. String fringe following the pattern (**figure 4**).

Fringe #1–2 and Fringe #24-25: 11º, 6.5 C, 11º

Fringe #3–4 and Fringe #22-23: 11º, 6.5 C, 11º, 6.5 V, 11º

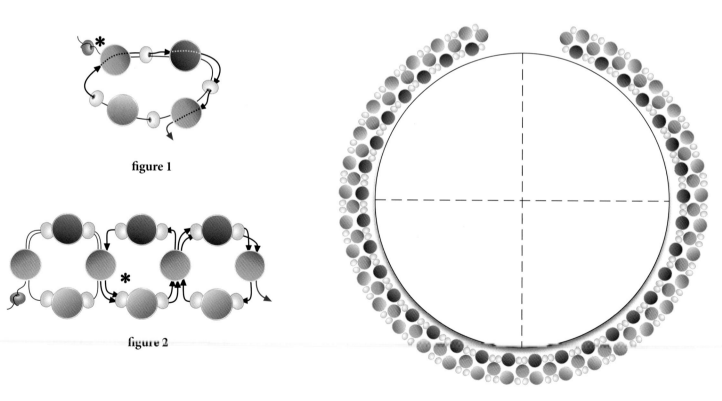

figure 1

figure 2

figure 3

Fringe #5 and Fringe #21: 11º, 6.5 C, 11º, 6.5 V, 11º, 10 CA, 11º

Fringe #6–7 and Fringe #19-20: 11º, 6.5 C, 11º, 6.5 V, 11º, 10 CA, 11º, 10 LC, 11º

Fringe #8–10 and Fringe #16-18: 11º, 6.5 C, 11º, 6.5 V, 11º, 10 CA, 11º, 10 LC, 11º, 14.5 C, 11º

Fringe #11–12 and Fringe #14–15: 11º, 6.5 C, 11º, 6.5 V, 11º, 10 CA, 11º, 10 LC, 11º, 14.5 C, 11º, 14.5 V, 11º

Center Fringe #13: 11º, 6.5 C, 11º, 6.5 V, 11º, 10 CA, 11º, 10 LC, 11º, 14.5 C, 11º, 14.5 V, 11º, focal bead or button

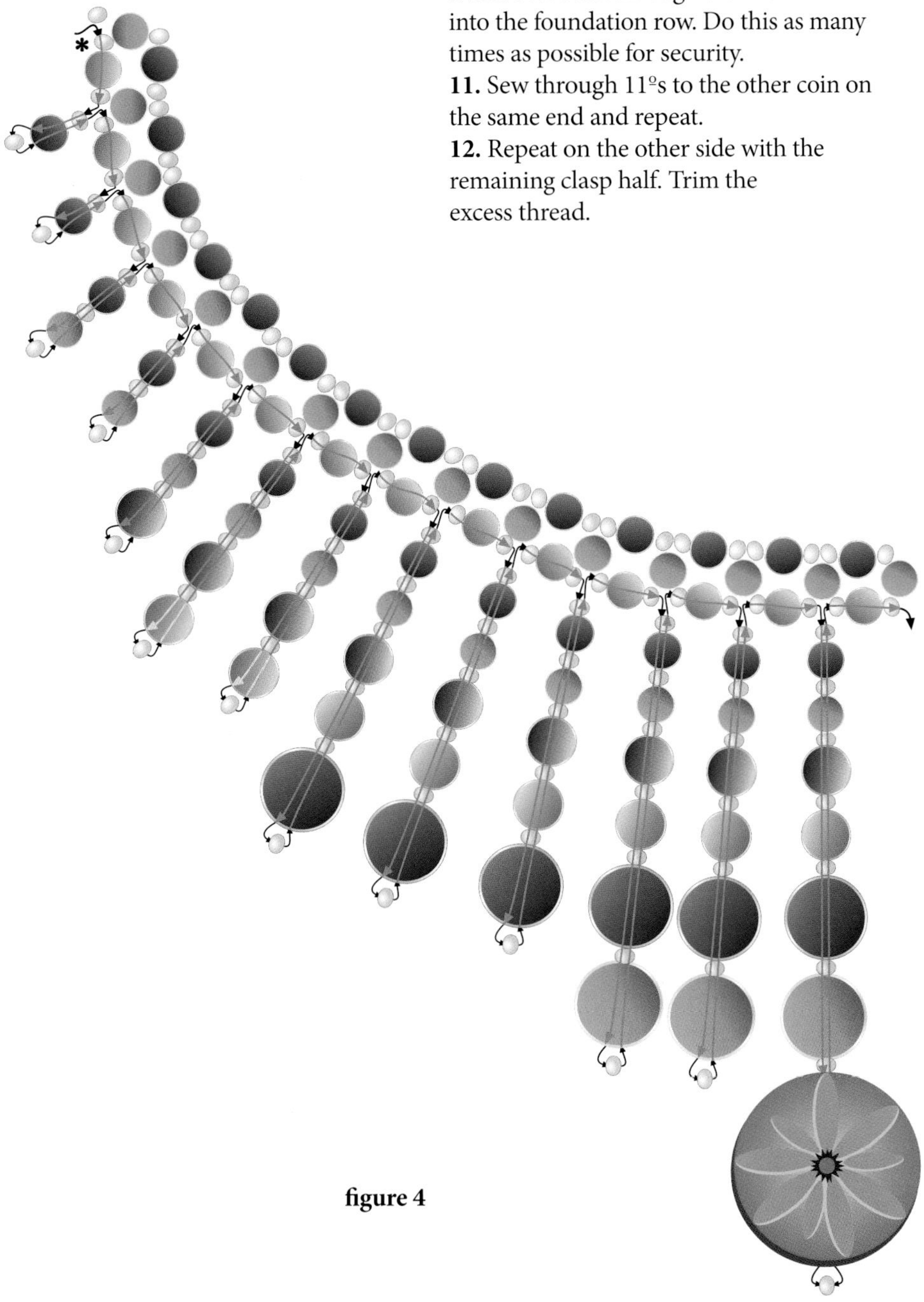

To use a large vintage button as your focal bead, mount it on leather as follows: Cut a hole in the center of a circular piece of leather, and sew a soldered jump ring to the leather. Glue the leather to the back of the button. Attach the button to the end of the fringe by looping through the jump ring several times. Sew back up through the fringe.

Attaching the clasp

10. Exit one of the end coins on the foundation row. Pick up five 11ºs, and wrap the thread around half the clasp loop twice. Sew back through the five 11ºs and into the foundation row. Do this as many times as possible for security.

11. Sew through 11ºs to the other coin on the same end and repeat.

12. Repeat on the other side with the remaining clasp half. Trim the excess thread.

figure 4

Yoli Pastuszak was introduced to the world of beading in 1999 by stringing rock chips on tigertail and a series of "never" statements. Fortunately, these never statements did not come to pass and she has moved on to seed beads, crystals, and a variety of color palettes. Yoli works and teaches at her local bead store. Visit her website, beadsiren.com.

Garden Haunt Necklace

I have lived in the Midwest for most of my life, so when I moved to northern Alabama five years ago, I was unprepared for its rich natural beauty. Northern Alabama is lush, green, and vibrant. The smell of flowers fills the air 10 months out of the year. The texture, complexity, and range of colors of even the smallest flowers and leaves are amazing and inspiring. As a result, my beadwork has become very organic and detailed.

Preparing the leaf pendant

1. Draw an outline of an elongated heart-shaped leaf on an index card. Place the focal bead on the top edge of the leaf. Check proportions, and adjust if necessary.

2. Cut out the leaf and place it on the Lacy's Stiff Stuff so its tip is 1 in. from the bottom center. Outline the leaf on the Lacy's using a fine-point marker.

3. Draw the central and side veins on the Lacy's.

4. Apply an even layer of epoxy to the focal bead and place it on the upper edge of the leaf as desired (**figure 1**). Dry for 30 minutes.

Embroidering the pendant

5. Thread a needle onto 2 yds. of thread and knot the end. Sew up through the Lacy's.

6. For the leaf's central vein, backstitch the following: Cs halfway down, Fs for the next quarter, and Ks for the remainder (**figure 2**).

7. Knot the thread on the back of the Lacy's. Sew up through the back of the Lacy's to the top of a leaf section where a side vein joins the central vein. Pick up one K and one F, and backstitch.

8. Backstitch the following: Fs for the first half of the vein and Ks for the second half. Repeat for all remaining veins except the bottom side veins.

9. Backstitch the bottom side veins with Ks. Knot the thread on the back of the Lacy's and cut.

stitch
bead embroidery, moss stitch, fringe
level
intermediate

supplies
- Flat-backed focal bead or cabochon, for example: carved mammoth netsuke, cabochon or tagua bat, animal, flower
- 8 mm faceted pearl
- 8º seed beads
  30 g A: dark olive luster
  15 g B: silver lined gold matte
  15 g C: olivine high luster
- 11º seed beads
  50 g D: army green matte
  25 g E: burnt orange topaz luster
  15 g F: olivine high luster
  10 g G: silver lined gold matte
- 15º seed beads
  20 g H: army green matte
  10 g I: dark olivine gold luster
  10 g J: burnt orange topaz luster
  10 g K: olivine high luster
  5 g L: silver lined gold matte
- **2** Size 2 hooks and eyes
- Nymo D or Superlon D thread, olive
- Size 12 beading needles
- 8½ x 11 piece Lacy's Stiff Stuff
- Ultrasuede to match
- Microcrystalline wax
- 5-min. epoxy glue
- Craft glue
- Olive fine-point permanent marker
- Blank 4 x 6 in. index cards
- White poster board
- Embroidery scissors

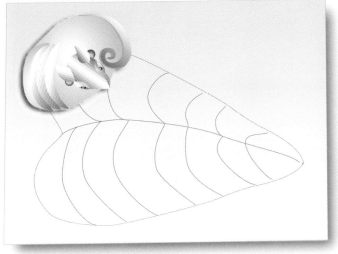

figure 1

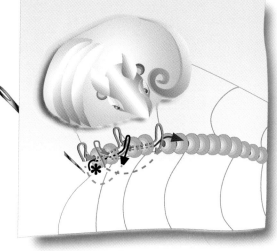

figure 2

10. Thread a needle onto 1½ yds. of thread, and knot the end. Sew up through the back of the Lacy's to the top of a leaf section where a side vein joins the central vein (**figure 3**).

11. Pick up one H, one I, and one H, and sew back down through the Lacy's about one bead's width away from the starting point to start the first moss stitch. This will cause the beads to lay with a picot.

12. Randomly continue to work with moss stitch using one H, one I, and one H to fill in the leaf. Knot the thread on the back and cut (**figure 3**).

13. Thread a needle onto 1½ yds. of thread, and knot the end. Sew up from the underside of the Lacy's where the moss stitch meets the focal bead. Backstitch around the back of the focal bead, picking up two Ds each time until reaching the moss stitch. Sew down through the Lacy's and through the last bead of the backstitch. Repeat for one more adjacent row. Anchor the thread on the back of the Lacy's, and cut (✳ **figure 3**).

14. Trim the Lacy's, leaving ⅛ in. around the leaf and focal bead.

15. Thread a needle onto 2 yds. of thread and knot the end.

16. If your focal doesn't have holes, go to Step 19. If your focal has holes, sew up through the back of the Lacy's and between the first and second D beads of the back-stitched row closest to the focal bead. Pick

up 15 or more Ds and sew down through the closest focal-bead hole. Anchor the thread to the back of the Lacy's (✳ **figure 3**).

17. Sew up through the Lacy's and the Ds (in the hole) to the point where the Ds are even with the top of the focal bead. Embellish the line of Ds with leaf, bud, flower, leaf, leaf, flower, leaf, leaf, and bud fringe, as described below. Continue the fringe pattern down the line of Ds until you reach the backstitched rows.

Leaf Fringe: Pick up five Ds and one H. Skip the H and sew through one D. Pick up three Ds. Sew through the first D of the leaf and the next D on the backstitched row (**figure 4**).

Flower Fringe: Pick up two Ds, one B, and one J. Skip the J and sew through the B and two Ds and then through the next D on the backstitched row (**figure 4**).

Bud Fringe: Pick up two Ds and three Gs. Skip the three Gs, and sew through two Ds and back through the next D on the backstitched row (**figure 4**).

18. Once the embellishment is complete, repeat Steps 16–17 through another hole in the focal bead (if available). Anchor the thread on the back of the Lacy's.

19. Sew through the second bead of the first backstitched row and continue the fringe pattern from Step 17 between the backstitched Ds.

20. Thread a needle onto 2 yds. of thread and knot the end. Sew up through the

back of the Lacy's near the focal bead. Sew a pearl on top of the moss stitch, and reinforce.

21. Sew up one bead width from the pearl and create a stack stitch. Pick up three Fs and one J (**figure 5**). Skip the J and sew through the three Fs and the Lacy's. Continue around the pearl.

22. Sew up from the back of the Lacy's and up through a stack. Sew through the J. Pick up one J and sew through the J at the top of the next stack. Repeat all the way around; keep the tension tight. Anchor the thread onto the back of the Lacy's (✳ **figure 5**).

23. Knot the end of the thread. Sew up from the back of the Lacy's through the first two beads of the stack closest to the focal bead (**figure 6**).

24. Create a leaf fringe, as in Step 17, using G's and one L.

25. Sew back down through the second F of the next stack.

26. Sew up from the back of the Lacy's and through the second bead of the stack just exited. Repeat adding leaf fringe around the pearl to the other side of the focal bead.

27. Apply a thin layer of glue to the pendant back. Place on the Ultrasuede glue-side down and press firmly. Smooth out any wrinkles or bubbles and dry overnight. (If the pendant is heavy, cut an index card to the shape of the pendant and glue it to the Lacy's. Dry overnight. Then glue the Ultrasuede to the back of the pendant.)

figure 3

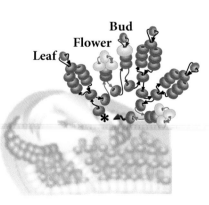

figure 4

figure 5

28. Trim the Ultrasuede even with the previously trimmed Lacy's.

29. Thread a needle onto 1½ yds. of thread, and knot the end. Position the needle between the Lacy's and the Ultrasuede. Sew through the edge of the Lacy's. Pick up two Ds and go back through the Ultrasuede. Go back through the bead. Pick up a second D, and repeat all the way around (**figure 7**).

Making the leaf clasp

30. Draw an outline of a 1¼ in. elongated heart-shaped leaf on an index card. Label "left" on one side. Turn over and label "right" on the other side. Place the leaf pattern left side up on a piece of Lacy's and outline with the marker. Mark the back of this leaf with an L. Repeat with the right side of the pattern.

31. Draw the central and side veins.

32. Beginning at the top of the central vein, backstitch Fs for three-fourths of the length and Ks for the rest.

33. For the remaining veins, backstitch the first half with Fs and the rest with Ks.

34. Follow Steps 11 and 12, and work in moss stitch between the veins.

35. Repeat Steps 31–34 for the second leaf.

36. Trim the Lacy's ⅛ in. around both leaves. Turn the leaves beaded-side down with the top of both leaves touching.

37. Place the hooks on the leaf marked left and the eyes on the leaf marked right and align them so they are directly opposite each other. Place the tops of the eyes about ¼ in. past the top edge of the left leaf and the tops of the hooks approximately ¼ in. past the top edge of the right leaf. Dab the hooks and eyes with craft glue to hold in place. Check the alignment, make the necessary adjustments, and dry.

38. Once the glue has dried, sew the eyes and hooks in place.

39. Cut two 2 x 2 in. squares of Ultrasuede.

40. On one square cut two small slits for the hooks. Apply craft glue to the back of the leaves. Slip the slits over the hooks. Dry for at least two hours.

41. Repeat Step 40 with the eyes.

Making the kinky multistrand necklace

42. Thread a needle onto 2 yds. of thread. Do not knot the end.

43. Pick up one leaf clasp with the tip pointing down. Find the center and count two edge beads over to the right. Anchor the thread with a knot on the top of the Lacy's, and sew through the edge bead, leaving a 48-in. tail.

44. Pick up one A and one D. Continue the pattern for 24 in., ending with an A. Secure with a stop bead on the end.

45. Thread a needle onto the 48-in. tail. Weave it through all the As, skipping the D's. Pull tightly to make it kink. Secure with a stop bead on the end. Set aside (**figure 8**).

46. Repeat the kinky fringe with another 2 yds. of thread anchored on the center edge bead.

47. Repeat the kinky fringe with another 2 yds. of thread on the second bead to the left of the center edge bead.

48. Repeat Steps 42–47 for the second leaf clasp.

49. Remove the stop beads from all of the strands, and check the tension. Tighten the tension if necessary. Temporarily attach the strands to the pendant by sewing through one edge bead. Add a stop bead, and check the balance of the pendant. Adjust the length by adding or removing beads to the shorter thread if necessary.

50. Bury the thread at the top of the Lacy's pendant and knot it. Come out of the edge bead below the edge bead entered. Sew through the first A and D (**figure 9**).

51. Make a berry cluster: Pick up three Es. Sew through the D that you just came out of and the next A.

52. Randomly add leaf and bud fringes (Step 17) and berry clusters. Always exit one of the Ds and then through the A on the strand. Randomly add berry clusters, always exiting the Ds.

53. Once reaching the end, sew through the second edge bead on the leaf clasps. Anchor the thread in the beadwork, and knot.

54. Repeat Steps 50–53 for the remaining five strands.

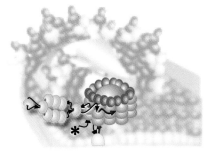

figure 6

figure 7

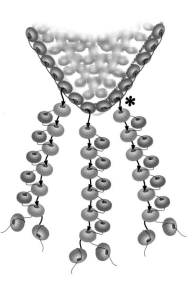

figure 8

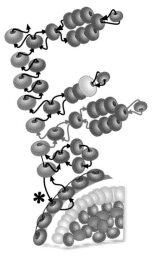

figure 9

Louise Hill graduated with a bachelor of fine arts degree in graphic design but left that field to pursue off-loom beadweaving as an art form. Since finding this passion for beading, her work has appeared in many art venues, books, and magazines and has won international awards. Visit louisehilldesigns.com.

Paradise Pendant

Florida's many qualities—miles of ocean coastline, bridges to the Keys, launches at Cape Canaveral, Miami architecture, Disney World, and most of all our unusual wildlife and vegetation—have inspired my beadwork. Even the less enjoyable experiences, like hurricanes, have found their way into my beads. My *Eyes of the Storms* purse was inspired by my experiences in the 2004 Florida hurricanes.

figure 1

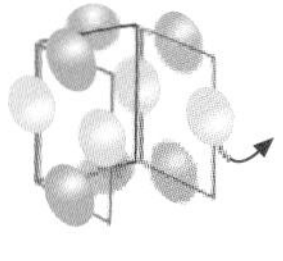

figure 3

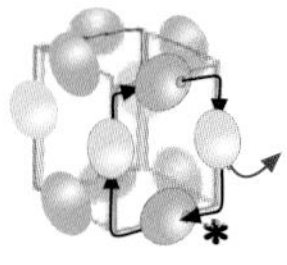

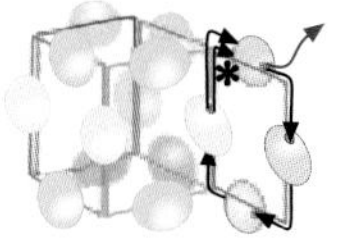

figure 5

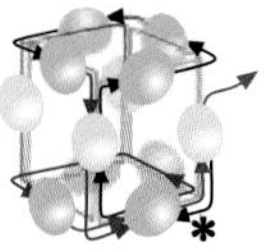

figure 7

figure 2

figure 4

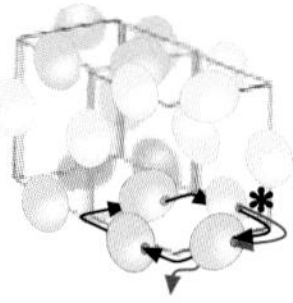

figure 6

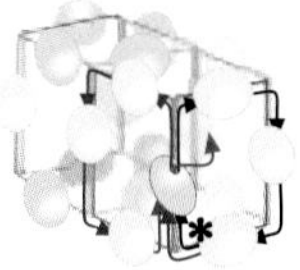

figure 8

stitches
cubic right-angle weave, right-angle weave, flat herringbone

level
advanced

supplies
House
- 3 mm SWAROVSKI ELEMENTS pearls
  - **426** A: gold
  - **118** B: light green
  - **200** C: copper
- 3 mm SWAROVSKI ELEMENTS bicones
  - **66** hyacinth
  - **55** fuchsia
- **200** 10° Japanese cylinder beads, D: matte metallic dark green iris
- **100** 11° Japanese cylinder beads E: matte metallic dark green iris
- **15** 10° Japanese cylinder beads F: opaque orange AB
- **15** 15° seed beads G: 24K gold plated
- 16 mm SWAROVSKI ELEMENTS rivolis, volcano
- FireLine 6-lb. test
- Size 12 beading needles
- Five-minute epoxy

Fringe
- SWAROVSKI ELEMENTS crystals in the following shapes and colors:
  - 3 mm bicones
    - **10** hyacinth
    - **12** fuchsia
  - **6** 4 mm bicones, hyacinth
  - 6 mm bicones
    - **2** hyacinth
    - **9** fuchsia
  - 8 mm bicones
    - **3** hyacinth
    - **1** fuchsia
- 3 mm SWAROVSKI ELEMENTS pearls
  - **36** copper
  - **122** light green
  - **135** gold

House base

1. Thread a needle onto 2 yds. of thread, leaving a 6-in. tail. Pick up four pearls: A, B, A, and B, and tie a square knot.

2. Stitch the first three sides of the cube with flat right-angle weave (RAW). Pull the thread tight (**figure 1**).

3. Fold the cube as shown (**figure 2**).

4. To complete the fourth side, pick up one B pearl on the bottom and top and go through all four pearls again, pulling tight to secure (**figure 3**).

5. Reinforce the cube by going back through all sides (**figure 4**).

6. All cubes share a side. To begin the next cube, pick up three A pearls and go through the pearl the thread is exiting to create the first side (**figure 5**).

7. Stitch the top side (**figure 6**) and bottom side (**figure 7**) of the new cube, picking up two new A pearls for each.

8. To complete the cube, pick up one A pearl. Reinforce the second cube by sewing through all sides (**figure 8**).

9. Follow the graph (**figure 9**) to complete Rows 1–10 to make the base of the house. Rows 1–2 are cubic RAW (**figure 10, a–c**). Start from the bottom, and work the first row of cubic RAW left to right using the pearls. At the end of the row, step up and work right to left. Rows 3–10 start and end with cubes. Stitch the center in flat RAW (**figure 11**).

> For cubic RAW, reinforce the cubes by following the thread paths (figure 4) and going back through the beadwork. The cubes need a tight tension to keep shape.

figure 9

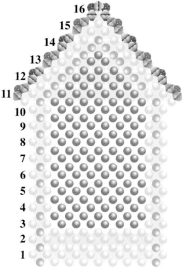

figure 10

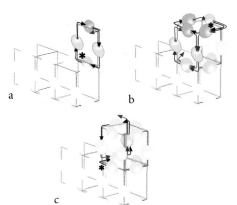

Row 3

figure 11

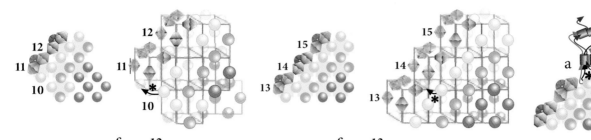

figure 12

figure 13

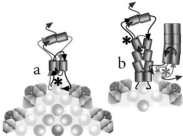

figure 14

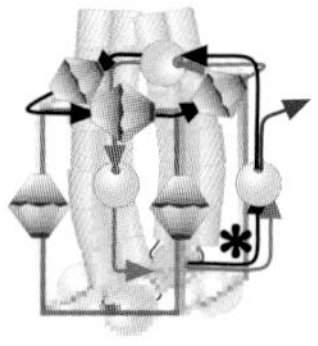

figure 15

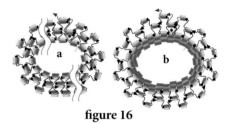

figure 16

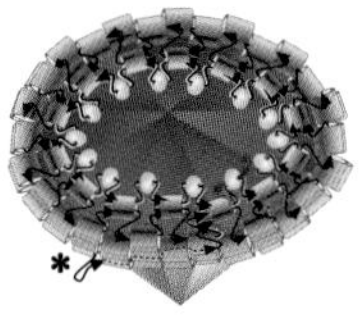

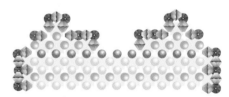

figure 17   figure 18

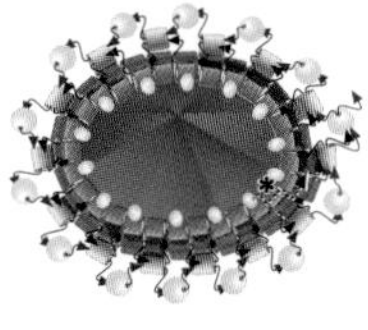

figure 19

figure 20

Roof

The roof is both cubic and flat RAW. Continue using the same thread.

10. Row 11 is an increase row. Increase at the end of Row 11 using crystals on the outer edge. Start by stitching the bottom side of the new cube (**figure 12**).

11. Decrease in Row 12. Work one cube from the end of the row using the pearls and crystals, and end with a decrease one cube before the end of the row (**figure 12**).

12. Work Rows 13–15 the same as Step 13. For Row 16, add the crystals at the top after the bail is completed (**figure 13**). End the thread.

Bail

13. Thread a needle onto 2 yds. of thread, leaving a 6-in. tail. Pick up two Ds. Secure the Ds to the pearl base and to each other to begin herringbone stitch (**figure 14a**).

14. Stitch 20 rows of flat herringbone with Ds. Secure the last row to the back pearl on top of the roof (**figure 14b**). Knot the thread but don't cut. Use the thread to secure the crystals at the top. Omit the back crystals. Knot the thread and end it (**figure 15**).

Bezeling the rivoli

15. Thread a needle onto 2 yds. of thread, leaving a 6-in. tail. Pick up 30 Ds. Go back through all the beads to form a circle, and tie a square knot. Work in even-count peyote stitch with Ds for four rows (**figure 16a**). Pull the ring tight.

16. Work in even-count peyote stitch for two rows with Es. Place the rivoli in the middle of the peyote stitch (front side up), and pull tight to form a cup to hold it (**figure 16b**). This is the back of the bezel.

17. Weave to the opposite side of the cup. Work one row in even-count peyote stitch using a row of Es. Work a row of even-count peyote stitch with Gs. Pull tight, and weave to the middle of two Es (**figure 17**).

18. Sew through one E on the bezel, pick up an F, and work peyote stitch through the next E in the cup all the way around (**figure 17**).

19. For the next row, peyote stitch all the way around with A pearls (**figure 18**).

20. Secure the thread, and hide the knot. Set the piece aside to be attached later.

Flower box

21. Thread a needle onto 1 yd. of thread, leaving a 6-in. tail. Follow the pattern (**figure 19**). Start from the bottom. Work the first row of cubic RAW left to right using the crystals and pearls. Step up and work right to left.

22. Once completed, secure the thread, and knot it. Set the flower box aside.

Making the fringe

23. Weave a length of thread into the first pearl on the house and secure. String a strand of fringe and attach to the last pearl of the house. Repeat. Once completed, tie the thread and cut it (**figure 20**).

Adding the rivoli

24. Thread a needle onto 1 yd. of thread, leaving a 6-in. tail. Secure the thread into the beadwork on the back of the rivoli.

25. Center the rivoli on the house. Sew through the open pearl holes on the house behind the rivoli to attach securely. Knot the thread, and cut it.

Adding the flower box

26. Mix epoxy and apply to each bead on the back of the flower box. Place on the house. The pearls sit in the valleys of the house. The top crystals rest on the fourth row from the bottom of the house. Make sure it is centered. Dry overnight.

27. Add a herringbone stitch chain with toggle closure.

Liz Thompson started beading about 15 years ago when she learned how to make a pair of earrings. The creative lightbulb went off, and she is currently exploring an unexplained love affair with bead embroidery. Liz has been published in the Alaskan Bead Society newsletter, Nicole Campanella's book *Flatwork*, *Bead&Button* magazine, and the *Bead-A-Day Calendar*. She has taught at a local bead store, at Henry Ford Community College, and is currently teaching at Stony Creek Bead in Ypsilanti, Mich. Liz has been a classroom assistant for a nationally known instructor at the *Bead&Button* Show for the past several years. Contact her at ethomps1@gmail.com or thebadliz.blogspot.com.

Starburst Necklace

Being a native Michiganian who has traveled and camped extensively throughout the state, I have looked in amazement at the urban settings in Detroit and in wonder at the natural surroundings in Tahquamenon Falls in the Upper Peninsula. I have used natural landscapes and cityscapes in my bead embroidery tapestries. Working with our local bead guild has given me exposure to many bead artists who come to Michigan to teach. With this experience, I have moved from using one bead stitch to another, then on to combining stitches and techniques. Living in a bead oasis in the metro Detroit area with many talented people around me has greatly increased my love, respect, and admiration for this art that has claimed me.

Covering the ring

1. Thread a needle onto 2 yds. of thread. Pick up four As and tie into a circle. Make a strip of four-bead right-angle weave (RAW) that is almost as long as the outer circumference of the ring, and wide enough to wrap around the ring (four to five units wide).
2. Once the strip is complete, sew it together around the ring by picking up one bead to connect the edges of the strip (**figure 1**).
3. Add additional RAW squares to the end of the strip to completely cover the ring, and join the ends together.

Embellishing the ring

4. On the top outer part of the ring, add a row of Bs between the RAW squares. Continue all the way around the ring. Peyote stitch a second row of Bs (**figure 2**).
5. Using Cs, stitch one row of peyote over the previous row (**figure 3**).
6. Sew down to the RAW base and position the needle in the very next row between two As. Pick up one E between each bead around the RAW (✳ **figure 3**).
7. Sew through the back of the ring's top just behind the embellishment rows from Step 4, exiting between two of the RAW As. Pick up one D between each bead around the base (**figure 4**). Repeat for a second row.

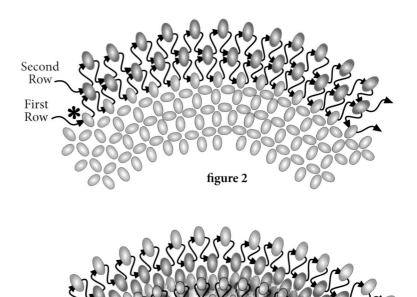

Second Row
First Row

figure 2

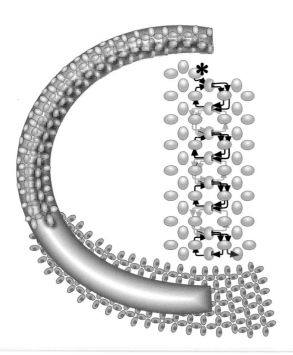

figure 1

figure 3

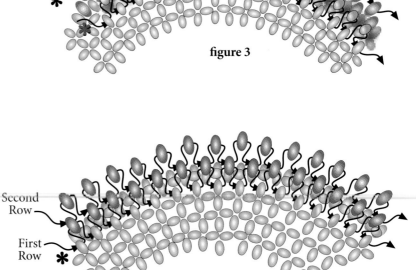

Second Row
First Row

figure 4

8. Work a three-bead picot with Ds between the beads in the previous peyote stitch row (**figure 5**).

9. Add 3 mm bicones between the middle beads of the picots (**figure 6**).

Making the bail

10. Thread a needle onto a comfortable length of thread. Pick up eight 11°s (color of choice or a combination). Work in even-count flat peyote for 32 rows. There will be 16 beads on each side of the bail. Zip one end of the bail to the base Ds on the back of the ring (**figure 7**).

11. Fold the bail in half, and stitch the other end to the next row of As on the back.

Making the Russian spiral rope chain

12. Thread a needle onto 3 yds. of thread. Pick up two Fs and one D. Repeat two more times for a total of nine beads. Sew through the beads again to form a circle, exiting the first F (**figure 8**).

13. Pick up one 11° and two 15°s. Skip two beads (15° and 11°), and sew through the following 15°. Repeat this all the way around. The row will spiral. Always sew through the next 15° of the current row, not the previous row (**figure 8**).

14. Substitute a 2 mm or 3 mm round crystal or 3 mm fire-polished bead for an 11° as desired (**figure 9**). Make the chain to the desired length. Finish with cones and a clasp.

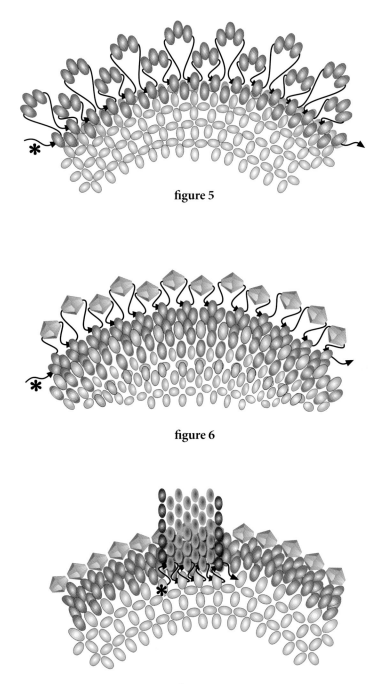

figure 5

figure 6

figure 7

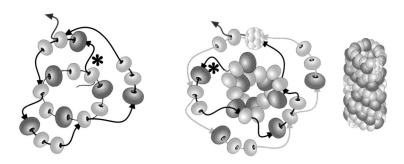

figure 8

figure 9

NanC Meinhardt, an accomplished artist, uses beads and off-loom beadweaving as her artistic medium. Her work is published in over 39 books and magazines including: *Masters: Beadweaving* (Lark 2008), *500 Beaded Objects* (Lark 2004), *The Art Of Beadwork* (Watson-Guptill 2005), *The Art and Elegance of Beadweaving* (Lark 2003), and *Creative Bead Weaving* (Lark 1998). NanC's beadwork has been exhibited at The Museum of Art and Design in New York, The Houston Center for Contemporary Craft, at numerous international shows, and can be viewed on her website, nancmeinhardt.com. NanC teaches internationally and is probably best known for her Master Class, "The Maze Project." NanC resides in Highland Park, Ill.

Rapunzel Lariat

The Midwest can be overlooked in favor of the two coasts, yet Illinois is more than a place to change planes. I live close to Chicago, the country's third-largest city. I visit often to take in the magnificent skyline, the Art Institute, the renowned architecture, world-class shopping, and the diversity of the many ethnic neighborhoods. Midwesterners take pride in tradition, continuity, and managing the rigors of winter. My beadwork is inspired by cherished seasonal memories: my mother's jewel-toned flower garden; bright Halloween costumes peeking from coats; my red snowsuit, yellow boots, and blue mittens in stark contrast to fresh white snow; and, at long last, spring and her soft, fragrant pastels. I love living in Illinois and I love making art. The two seem to go hand in hand.

stitches
flat peyote, two-drop peyote, netting
level
intermediate

supplies
Be creative and make the piece your own. Use this supply list as a suggestion, rather than a list of "must haves."

- 11º seed beads, **10 g** each of
  A: matte dark gold bronze
  B: gold bronze
  C: silver lined root beer AB
  D: dark gold
  E: light gold
- 8º seed beads, **10 g** each of three colors similar or contrasting palette to the 11ºs
- 15º seed beads, **10 g** each of three colors similar or contrasting palette to the 11ºs
- Embellishment beads: two colors of freshwater pearls, center-drilled keshi pearls, 5 mm pinch beads, sequins, 3 mm and 4 mm fire-polished beads, SWAROVSKI ELEMENTS bicones, ½ hank 13º charlottes, a mix of flowers, leaves, teardrops, lentils and daggers. (Use any mix and as much as desired. This is a great place for those leftover beads.)
- Size 12 beading needles
- Thread: Silamide size A, FireLine 6-lb. test, or Wildfire

Stitching the foundation row (use 11ºs)

1. Thread a needle onto a comfortable length of thread. Pick up two As, leaving a 6-in. tail. Sew back through the first A to form a two-bead ladder. The working thread and the tail will exit the same A in opposite directions (**figure 1**).
2. Pick up three Bs. Sew down through #2, up through #1, and diagonally up through #4 (**figure 1**).
3. Pick up two As (#5 and #6). Sew through the two #3s treating the two beads as one. Sew up through #4 and from left to right diagonally through #6 (**figure 2**).

Keep bead 1 (with the tail) on the left for the foundation row. If you are left handed, reverse all thread paths.

4. Repeat Steps 2–3 for 38–40 in. End with two As. Some of the length will be taken up when you embellish the lariat (**figure 3**).

To keep the lariat spiraling in the same direction, don't reverse the thread path. If the thread path is reversed, four beads will line up straight as in square stitch.

Stitching rows 2–4

5. Turn the work to the side. Pick up two C's. Skip one bead and sew through two As. Work in two-drop peyote with Cs going through two As on the previous row. Continue for the length of the lariat (**figure 4**).
6. Stitch another row of two-drop peyote, going through two Cs on the previous row. Vary the colors from end to end (**figure 4**).
7. Stitch a row of regular peyote stitch with 8ºs by sewing through two 11ºs of the previous row as before. Keep the tension tight, tie half-hitch knots every few stitches and coil the beadwork to help the piece spiral. For interest, use a variety of the three colors of 8ºs. Think of the piece as three sections and use a different color 8º in each section (**figure 5**).

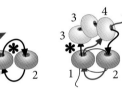

figure 1

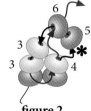

figure 2

figure 3

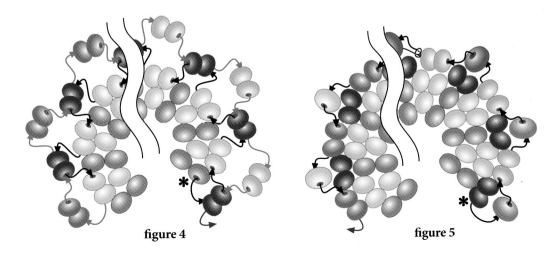

figure 4

figure 5

Embellishing the lariat

8. Begin the next row by tying half-hitch knots and sewing through the last two 11ºs at the end. Sew through the first 8º going towards the center of the lariat. Pick up two 15ºs, one pearl or fire-polished bead, and two 15ºs. Sew through the next 8º. Use more or fewer beads depending on the space between the 8ºs Use different colors of pearls, fire-polished beads, and 15ºs that will coordinate with the 8ºs in each section. Repeat a minimum of 35 times at one end **(figure 6a)**.

9. Change the embellishment to five 15ºs through the middle portion of the lariat **(figure 6b)**.

10. Repeat Step 9 on the other end of the lariat **(figure 6c)** varying the color of beads on this end.

11. Add a second row of embellishment on each end of the lariat by either using similar combinations as in Step 9, creating a row of netting between the focal beads of the previous row **(figure 7a)**; or, adding a second layer of embellishment over the first between the 8ºs of the previous row, using different focal beads **(figure 7b)**.

12. Once the two rows of embellishment are completed, further embellish the end of the lariat by adding 4 mm fire-polished beads, pearls, or crystals. Pick up a couple of 15ºs on each side of the larger beads. Finish the piece creatively.

13. Arrange the lariat as a continuous spiral or allow it to take its own shape.

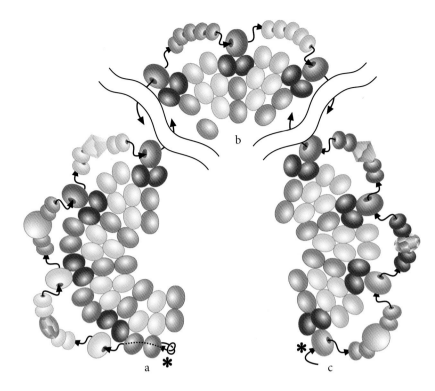

figure 6

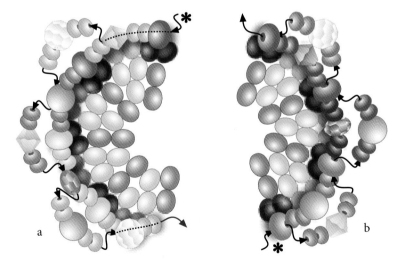

figure 7

Diane Hyde has been making jewelry, wearable art, dolls, and purses since the 1970s. Her vintage-look jewelry has appeared in galleries, at fine art shows, at Von Maur Department Stores, in a nationally distributed catalog, at trunk shows for Nordstrom, and in published magazine articles. Recently, bead embroidery and exploring combinations of unexpected objects, vintage components, and imagery have become a main focus. This exploration created a new genre—a bit Victorian, a bit eclectic, and nostalgic. Patterned after "Steampunk," but with the addition of bead embroidered seed beads, pearls, and crystals, the genre has become "Beadpunk." Visit designersfindings.net.

Wisconsin Memories 1952

Wisconsin to me is nostalgia. In the 1950s, our family vacations were often to Wisconsin. I still remember the joy of wiggling my toes in the warm sand at lake's edge and looking for minnows. We stayed in quaint rental cabins that lined every lake in the state in those days. Old black-and-white vacation photos still make me smile, while their monochromatic tones and images inspire both my color palette and my melancholy. I'm equally inspired by the rich history of this state, so visible everywhere: Milwaukee's beautiful historic buildings; the fabulous old mansions on the bluffs overlooking Lake Michigan; the warm, friendly people—many descendants of European settlers—and the hundreds of charming little towns and dairy farms that dot this green and rolling state. My grandfather was born in the small town of Wild Rose. I'm sure he'd be happy to know I ended up living here in Wisconsin—a wonderful place to call home.

stitch
bead embroidery
level
intermediate

supplies
- 8º seed beads
  - **2 g** A: pewter matte
  - **.5 g** B: bronze shiny
- 11º seed beads
  - **2 g** C: pewter matte
  - **2 g** D: bronze shiny
  - **1 g** E: silver nickel shiny
- 15º seed beads
  - **3 g** F: silver nickel shiny
  - **2 g** G: pewter matte
  - **.5 g** H: bronze shiny
- 1.8 mm micro-cube beads (Out On A Whim)
  - **2 g** bronze matte
  - **2 g** pewter matte
- SWAROVSKI ELEMENTS crystals
  - **54** 3 mm bicones, dorado 2X
  - **3–18** 4 mm bicones, dorado 2X
  - 6 mm two-loop crystal connector, black diamond
- SWAROVSKI ELEMENTS pearls
  - 10 mm light grey
  - **26** 8 mm antique brass
  - **2** 8 mm light grey
  - **42** 6 mm antique brass
  - **15** 5 mm light grey
  - **6** 5 mm antique brass
  - **12** 4 mm light gray
  - **5** 4 mm antique brass
  - **6** 3 mm antique brass
  - 3 mm light grey
- Assortment of charms
- Assortment of metal stampings
- 32 x 14 mm bottle
- **2** typewriter keys
- Cut-off key (Gary Wilson Lapidary)

- Watch parts
  - ⅜-in. diameter watch plate
  - **2** smaller watch plates
  - 18 mm diameter gear
  - assorted 8–12 mm gears
  - Ladies watch case to hold parts
  - Watch face
  - Tiny parts and gears to fill bottle
- Chain (Designer's Findings)
  - 8–22 in. 9 x 19 mm oval link
  - 12–16 in. 4 mm link, antique silver
  - 6 in. 2 x 5 mm oval link, antique brass
- Jump rings
  - **8–10** 2 x 3 mm oval, antique brass and antique silver
  - **8–10** 3 x 4 mm oval, antique brass and antique silver
  - **8–10** 4 x 5 mm oval, antique brass and antique silver
- Soldered jump rings (or split rings)
  - **8–12** 5 mm, brass and silver
  - **16–20** 6 mm, brass and silver
- **16–18** 2 mm crimp beads, brass or silver
- Krylon Preserve It! matte or gloss spray sealer or decoupage medium
- Spray Mount adhesive
- E-6000 glue
- Beadalon knotting glue
- 6 x 6 in. Lacy's Stiff Stuff
- Brass blank or medium card stock (for mounting the image)
- Nymo D thread, brown and grey
- FireLine, 6-lb. test
- Flexible beading wire, .014 clear
- Ultrasuede
- Size 10, 12, and 13 beading needles
- Drill

For all watch parts, gears, typewriter keys, etc., search Beadpunk.net, Etsy, or eBay.

Preparation

1. Scan or photocopy a photo and resize as desired. Print on medium-weight paper. For the backing, choose a brass blank, used here, or medium cardstock cut to fit the desired photo.
2. Use Spray Mount adhesive to attach the photo to the backing. Seal with Krylon Preserve It! or decoupage medium.
3. Plan the placement of the lower half of the necklace by arranging the photo, the large watch plate, other watch pieces, a typewriter key, stampings, etc. in a pleasing design. Once you are satisfied, take a photo of the layout to serve as a reference during assembly.
4. There are three components that will be embellished with bead embroidery—the focal piece and two connectors. Assemble these elements on Lacy's Stiff Stuff. Position overlapping components precisely to create a unified design. Adhere with E-6000 glue. Trim the excess Lacy's, leaving a ¼ in. border. Dry for one hour.

Embellishing the focal piece (figure 1)

5. Work four rows of backstitch and decorative edging, following the photo for inspiration, choosing beads and bead placements that suit your design. Beads used in **Round 1**: Ds, As, an 8 mm antique brass pearl with an H stopper, and Bs. **Round 2**: 3 mm matte pewter cubes, 8 mm pearls, 4 mm pearls, 6 mm pearls, 3 mm pearls, bronze micro cubes, Hs. **Round 3**: Fs, Gs (interchange every few beads), 3 mm Dorado 2X crystals, Hs, Fs and for the picot, Ds and Hs. **Round 4**: 3 mm bicones, As, Hs, 4 mm bicones with 15º tops, picot edging using F, E, F.
6. When the embroidery is complete, trim the Lacy's and color the edge with permanent marker.

Embellishing connector 1 (figure 2)

7. Thread a needle onto 12 in. of FireLine, and knot one end. Cut a ¼-in. Ultrasuede circle, and sew through back to front.
8. Sew through a hole in a small curved watch plate, back to front, pulling the Ultrasuede circle snug against the back

figure 1

figure 2

figure 3

figure 4

of the plate. Pick up a metal leaf charm, a flower charm, and an 11º stopper. Skip the 11º and go back through all beads, charms, the watch plate, and the Ultrasuede. Pull snug, then go through all beads and components again to reinforce. Anchor the thread in the Ultrasuede, tie it off with half-hitch knots, and cut.

9. Trim the Ultrasuede circle to a 5 mm diameter. Add a drop of glue to the thread hidden inside to secure.

10. Cut a 1-in. circle of Ultrasuede. Glue an old typewriter key to it using E-6000 and dry for one hour.

11. Thread a needle onto 16 in. of FireLine, and knot one end. Insert the needle next to the edge of the typewriter key. Backstitch around it with Ds. Trim the Ultrasuede backing to the edge of the beads. Glue it to the watch plate with E-6000, and let it dry for one hour.

12. Thread a needle onto 8 in. of FireLine and sew through a soldered jump ring. Sew through the top hole of the curved watch plate from back to front, leaving a

3-in. tail. Pick up one 3 mm pearl, and go back through the watch plate hole.

13. Knot the tail, trim, and glue. Repeat Step 12 at the other end of the watch plate.

Embellishing connector 2 (figure 3)

14. Glue a typewriter key and a compatible watch plate to a piece of Lacy's Stiff Stuff with E-6000. Leave a ¼ in. space between and around the pieces. Dry for one hour.

15. Thread a needle onto 12 in. of FireLine, and knot one end. Using As, surround the key with the holes facing outward.

16. At the top edge of the watch plate, backstitch a row of bronze micro cubes. Backstitch around the remainder of the watch plate randomly with Fs, Gs, and Hs. Sew on pearls, beads, and charms through the watch-plate holes as desired.

17. Continue backstitching around the typewriter key. Begin with shiny bronze micro cubes on the left and graduate to matte bronze micro cubes on the right. For the next row, alternate three 15ºs and three

11ºs all the way around, varying the colors in the sequence.

18. Pick up 3 mm bicones with an F as a picot between the As and the bronze micro cube beads on the side and top portions of the typewriter key. Trim the excess Lacy's. Color the edges with permanent marker.

Assembling the necklace

19. Lay out the finished bead components and other items you have chosen to connect in the design.

20. Whip stitch two 5 mm soldered jump rings or split rings to the Lacy's on each end of Connector 2. Whip stitch two 5 mm soldered jump rings or split rings to the top edge of the focal piece, placing them about 1 in. apart (**figure 4**).

21. Whip stitch 8–10 5 mm soldered jump rings or split rings to the bottom edge of the focal piece. Bury the thread, and cut.

22. Attach small charms with jump rings to the rings at the bottom edge of the focal piece, leaving the two center rings unembellished (**figure 5**).

figure 5

figure 6

23. Drill any components that need holes. Connect with oval jump rings to split rings using various sizes to fit each piece.

24. Attach a woman's watch case filled with small parts to the top of Connector 1 with medium jump rings.

25. Connect the top of the watch case to a connector made by sewing the 6 mm two-loop crystal connector over the 14 mm ring gear.

26. Make an 18 mm watch gear connector by sewing a pearl to the center of the gear. Attach it to the bottom of Connector 1 with two jump rings. Pick up one 2-in. piece of brass chain at the bottom left section of Connector 1, draping down and connecting to the side of the gear.

27. Connect the bottom of the gear to the top left of the focal bead piece (**figure 4**).

28. Connect the key to the top of Connector 2 using two 1-in. pieces of silver round-link chain. Connect the small wing to the bottom of Connector 2 with medium jump rings.

29. Connect the bottom of the wing to the top right of the focal piece. Connect the gear to the top left of the focal piece (**figure 4**).

Making and attaching the pendant bottle

30. Fill a small bottle with watch parts (time in a bottle). Glue an 8 mm light gray

pearl over the top hole. Peyote stitch a strip of micro cubes two beads wide around the bottle neck. Make a three-bead picot at the top using Fs. Make a picot edge at the bottom through every other micro cube using 3 mm Dorado 2X with Fs as a picot.

31. Sew split rings to each side of the peyote strip of micro cubes. Cut two 1-in. pieces of small oval link chain. Attach one chain to each split ring on the bottle's neck using small oval jump rings. Sew the other two ends onto the Lacy's at the bottom back of the focal piece (**figures 5 and 6**).

Attach the backing

32. Cut a piece of Ultrasuede shaped to fit the backs of the focal piece and Connector 2. Attach to the edge of the Lacy's using tiny stitches. Trim off any extra Ultrasuede. Once the backing is applied, use available holes in the watch plate to glue in the stems of watch gears with E-6000. Watch dials may also be used (**figure 8**).

Making and attaching the necklace strands

33. Many types of necklace strands can go with this design from chain to strung pearls and crystals, to beaded spiral rope. Follow the photo of the necklace or make your own design.

figure 7

figure 8

Diane Fitzgerald teaches internationally and has authored 10 books about beadwork, most recently, *Shaped Beadwork* (Lark 2009). Her articles and images of her work have appeared in numerous books and magazines. In 2008, she received the "Excellence in Beadwork" award at the *Bead&Button* Show. Learn more about Diane and her work at dianefitzgerald.com.

Crystal Helix Beaded Bead

stitch
looped Zulu
level
intermediate

supplies (for one bead)

- **1 g** 15º seed beads
- **70** 3 mm SWAROVSKI ELEMENTS bicones
- 12 mm wooden bead with ⅛-in. hole
- FireLine 6-lb. test
- Size 12 beading needles
- Gold nail polish (or color of choice)
- ⅛-in. diameter wooden dowel about 8 in. long
- 3 in. masking tape
- Microcrystalline wax
- Lighter or Thread Zapper

I have the advantage of living in Minnesota, a state which boasts a rich maze of fiber arts networks—weavers, embroiderers, quilters, sewers, lace makers, basket makers, and of course, beaders. Many are linked through the Textile Center of Minnesota, a supportive source that educates and promotes these artisans through exhibits, classes, a library, and meeting space.

Preparing the wooden bead

1. Paint the wooden bead with two coats of nail polish, drying between coats.

2. Wrap the masking tape around the dowel about 3 in. from one end.

Embellishing the wooden bead

3. Thread a needle onto 2 yds. of thread, double, wax, and knot. Clip the tail 1 mm from the knot, and melt it with a lighter or Thread Zapper.

Row 1: Pick up 14 15º seed beads. Push the 15ºs to within 1 in. of the knot. Separate the strands between the beads and the knot. Sew between the strands, and pull tight to form a tight ring. Sew back through the last two 15ºs strung (**figure 1**).

Row 2: Pick up one bicone and three 15ºs. Push the beads into place against the ring. Position the needle between the fourth and fifth beads on the ring. Sew up under the thread of the ring towards the inside (**figure 2**). Pull the thread until you hear it "snap" into place, and pull tight. With your thumb, push the bicone up to the left so it sits against the previous bead.

To hold the bead while working, place it onto the dowel above the masking tape. Continue to add loops, shaping the beadwork around the wooden bead (figure 3).

Row 3: For the next loop, pick up two bicones and three 15ºs. Sew up under the thread between the sixth and seventh bead of the ring (**figure 4**).

4. Add four more loops of two bicones and three 15ºs, attaching each loop after the next two seed beads, counting from where the last loop was connected. There will be two 15ºs left on the ring (**figure 4**).

5. Pick up two bicones and three 15ºs. Sew upward under the next loop, anchoring the thread so it hangs between the bicone and the 15º (like a step up) (**figure 5**).

Remaining spiral loops

6. Pick up two bicones and three 15ºs. Sew upward under the next loop, anchoring the thread between the second bicone and the next 15º (**figure 6**).

7. Repeat until there are 10 sets of bicones in each spiral row around the wooden bead except the first spiral row which will have nine (**figure 7**).

Tight tension and well waxed thread prevent the thread from slipping out of the loops.

8. Pick up one bicone and two 15ºs. Sew up under the next loop, anchoring the thread so that it hangs between the bicone and the first 15º. There will now be 10 bicones in each spiral row (**figure 8**).

9. To finish, pick up one 15º and sew through the first 15º after the crystal in each of the seven loops. Pass through the 15ºs a second time if possible (**figure 8**). Knot the thread, and weave in the tails.

Completing the necklace

10. Make 17 beaded beads. String, alternating with 10 mm gold beads. Attach a clasp half to each end of the necklace, and finish off.

figure 1

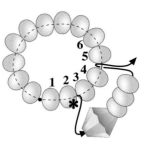

figure 2

figure 3

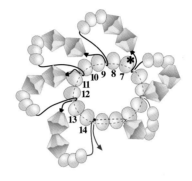

figure 4

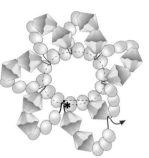

figure 5

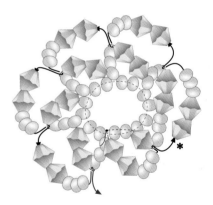

figure 6

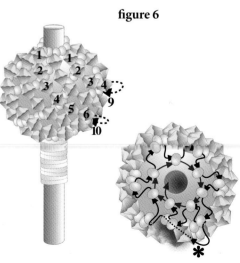

figure 7   **figure 8**

Darcy Horn is the sole creator of each piece of art-to-wear produced from her studio. She personally selects each component that goes into a finished work. Her preferred beadwork methods are bead embroidery and free-form peyote because they can ideally convey her creativity to its fullest. "Beadwork is the best medium I have found where what I visualize, what my mind's eye sees, my hands can recreate," says Darcy. "I rarely begin a project with absolute surety of the finished piece. I assemble a palette of beads, but allow the work to develop organically as I stitch." Visit thejadedog.com for more of Darcy's work.

Free-Form Bracelet

I am most influenced by collage artists and photographers, particularly Dave McKean and Nick Bantock, for composition. For structure and balance I turn to my study of architecture, especially that of Corbusier and Gaudi. I am also inspired by sound, smells, people, and landscapes of the Northwest and Southwest. When someone wears my work, I want them to feel like they are part of a living sculpture. My designs enhance and accentuate the wearer's uniqueness and individuality.

stitches
peyote, brick
level
intermediate

supplies
- **1–10 g** each of seed beads in sizes 6º to 15º in any combination including: cylinder beads, hex-cuts, triangles, squares, charlottes, and Japanese and Czech seed beads
- **3–11** 20–30 mm cabochons or buttons (in different sizes)
- **3–11** accent beads (18 mm or smaller) in varying sizes and shapes: pearls, crystals, metals, stones, pressed glass
- Size 12 beading needles
- **2** buttons (for the clasp)
- FireLine, 6-lb. or 8-lb. test
- Scrap paper or bead mat
- Ruler

Planning the design

1. Assemble a palette of beads for possible use. On scrap paper or a bead mat, draw a shape the desired length and width of the piece. Possible shapes include a rectangle, parallelogram, or a rounded edge rectangle. This is a template for the finished outer shape of the bracelet. This bracelet is a 7 x 3-in. parallelogram.

Bezeling the cabochons

2. Thread a needle onto 3 ft. of thread. Pick up an even number of 11º round seed beads or 11º cylinder beads and create a ring that will fit around one of the cabochons. Leave a short tail. Using circular even-count peyote stitch, complete as many rows as needed to create a bezel that fits a cabochon. Insert the cabochon into the beadwork. Tighten the bezel by using 15º seed beads for the last row(s) on the top of the cabochon (**figure 1**).

3. Weave back to the first row. Stitch two or three rows of peyote stitch with 15's to enclose the back of the bezel. Secure the threads and tails with half-hitch knots.

4. Repeat Steps 2 and 3 to bezel the remaining cabochons (**figure 2**).

5. Arrange the cabochons, accent beads, and buttons within the template, and arrange the palette of seed beads (**figure 2**).

Connecting the accent beads

6. Using peyote stitch, connect the cabochons and accent beads. Don't be afraid to graduate the size of beads and use a mix of colors. The beads should twist and turn (**figure 2**).

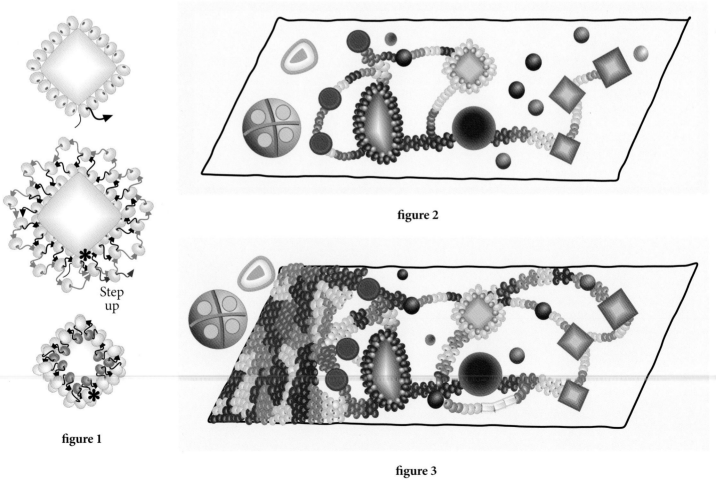

figure 1

figure 2

figure 3

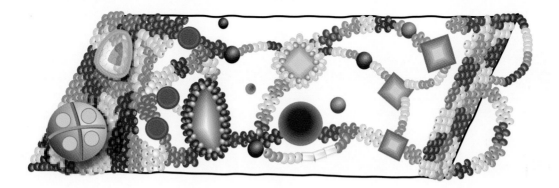

figure 4

Working the piece

7. Once the cabochons are initially connected with a web of peyote stitch, slide the buttons off the template. Work in brick stitch to create a solid fabric of beads on both ends of the bracelet. Vary the bead colors, sizes, and shapes as desired **(figure 3)**.

8. Change to peyote stitch to fill in the middle of the bracelet, continuing the web-like structure **(figure 3)**.

9. Connect the existing branches with peyote or brick stitch using seed beads of your choice. The bracelet can be solid or lacy.

10. Extend the beadwork towards the sides of the bracelet to fill out the template's shape.

11. Let the beads be the guide. Never force the needle into the beadwork. Don't force the work to be flat or straight. Some sections may need to be zipped together.

Creating the clasp

12. Attach two buttons on one end of the bracelet. Sew through the buttons several times, then sew through the piece. Secure with half-hitch knots **(figure 4)**.

13. On the opposite side of the bracelet make button loops. Starting on the outer edge, pick up enough beads of different shapes and sizes to fit over the buttons.

Sew through a spot in the outer edge that corresponds with the button on the opposite side. Work in peyote stitch over these beads for several rows. Repeat to make a second loop **(figure 4)**.

Finishing the bracelet

14. Look at the piece. Are there bare patches, not enough texture, missing colors, or visible thread? Add the desired elements.

15. Add fringe to the piece, if desired, using a variety of seed beads for texture. Pick up accent beads if desired, to fill in gaps.

Marcia Laging Cummings is intrigued by antique glass beads, and because of this interest became a collector and occasional bead stringer. Years later she discovered the work of Joyce Scott. That led to big trouble: an affair with seed beads. Marcia's beadwork has twice received a Juror's Merit award in the Dairy Barn Bead International shows, an art exhibition that draws nearly 15,000 visitors each year. Her work has been published in *500 Beaded Objects* (Lark 2004) and *The Art of Beaded Beads* (Lark 2010). She has shown beadwork in several *Bead&Button Show* Bead Dreams exhibits and a variety of other venues. Contact Marcia at garlicvino@aol.com.

Black & White & Red All Over
(With a Splash of Lime) Necklace

Every spring thousands of migrating red-capped sandhill cranes fly over central Nebraska, stopping to rest and hang out on the river, producing a magnificent avian display. Every fall another sort of migration fills my hometown of Lincoln with a sea of red as thousands of Cornhusker football fans gather. In beading this necklace I tried a Nebraska red-inspired color experiment with Kool-aid (originally created in 1927 in Hastings, Neb., by Edwin Perkins). I knew that it could be used as a dye in felting so I experimented using cherry Kool-Aid to dye my thread. I did use the thread in this piece, however, take my advice: If you want red thread, buy red thread. Add sweetener and water and drink the Kool-Aid.

stitches
right-angle weave, peyote, square
level
intermediate

supplies
- 11º Japanese seed beads,
  28 g each of
    A: opaque red
    B: black
    C: white
- **80** 11º Japanese seed beads
  D: lime green
- **80** 8º Japanese or Czech seed beads, lime green
- 15 mm red drop bead or pendant
- **2** 10 mm round red beads or 8 mm light Siam SWAROVSKI ELEMENTS round crystals
- **2** 10 mm flat lime green side-drilled lentils
- **2** 4 mm light Siam SWAROVSKI ELEMENTS bicones
- Nymo D thread, red and white
- Size 12 beading needles
- Wax

Dyeing with Kool-Aid only works with protein fibers. Search for online directions, if you are interested.

Diagonal right-angle weave squares

1. Thread a needle onto 3 yds. of white thread, and condition it. Pick up four B 11ºs, and make the first right-angle weave (RAW) square by sewing through the first bead strung.
2. Continue across the row following this color sequence: one B and two Cs; three Cs; one C and two Bs; three Bs; one C and two Bs; three Bs (**figure 1**).
3. Follow the RAW pattern, making sure there are seven vertical 11ºs at the top and bottom of each row to complete the square (**figure 2**).
4. Make 10 squares.

Peyote checkerboards

5. Thread a needle onto 5 ft. of white thread. Pick up five Cs, five Bs, five Cs, and five Bs (**figure 3**).
6. Stitch even-count peyote following the peyote graph.
7. Make two checkerboards.

Square stitch arcs

8. Thread a needle onto two yds. of thread. Pick up 10 Ds, searching for the narrowest beads. Square stitch one row (**figure 4**).
9. Stitch two more rows using 8ºs, using the widest 8ºs in the fourth row. Each arc consists of four rows of square stitch.
10. Make four arcs.

Square stitch center component

11. Thread a needle onto 2 yds. of red thread. Pick up eleven As, and square stitch for 14 rows.
12. On Row 15 decrease to nine As by dropping an A on each end (**figure 5a**).
13. On Row 16 decrease to seven As by dropping an A on each end (**figure 5b**).
14. On Row 17 decrease to five As by dropping an A on each end (**figure 5c**).
15. On Row 18 decrease to three As by dropping an A on each end. The final row will have only one bead (**figure 5d**).

figure 1

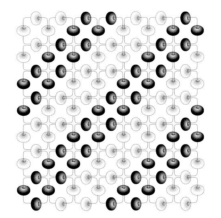

figure 2

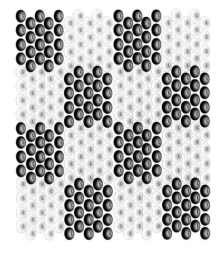

figure 3

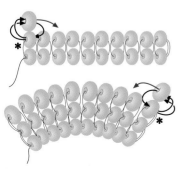

figure 4

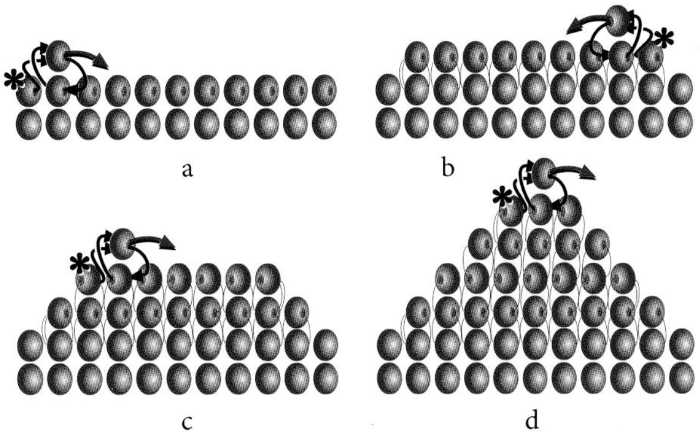

figure 5

Right-angle weave neckband

16. Thread a needle onto 3 yds. of red thread. Pick up four As and tie into a ring. Sew through the first three As again.
17. Pick up three As and work in RAW. Continue in RAW until there are seven squares in the first row.
18. Continue in RAW with As until the piece is 20 in. long.

Attaching the components

19. Attach one checkerboard to one diagonal square by zipping the vertical beads of the RAW into the peyote stitch (✴ **figure 6**).
20. Attach the second diagonal square to the outside of the first diagonal square to form an arrow shape. Attach the squares using RAW. Pick up one new 11º, following the pattern, as the bottom and top of each RAW square using a right and left bead from each square (✴ **figure 6**).
21. Attach one arc into the corner by sewing beads of the arc into the vertical beads of the diagonal square and the checkerboard (✴ **figure 6**).
22. Attach the third diagonal square on top of the second (outer) diagonal square, forming an arrow. Using RAW, pick up one new 11º for the right and left of each RAW square, with the top bead from the second diagonal square and the bottom bead from the third diagonal square (✴ **figure 7**).
23. Attach the fourth diagonal square to the outside of the third square, forming an arrow. Using RAW, pick up one new 11º for the bottom and top of each RAW unit using a right and left bead from each square (✴ **figure 7**).
24. Attach the fifth diagonal square to the top of the fourth diagonal square, forming an arrow. Using RAW, pick up one new 11º bead for the right and left bead of each RAW square using a top and bottom bead from each diagonal square (✴ **figure 7**).
25. Sew 10 mm round beads and 10 mm flat lentils on as indicated (✴ **figure 7**).
26. Sew another arc into the corner by sewing the arc beads into the vertical beads of the diagonal RAW squares ✴ (**figure 7**).
27. Attach the top of the fifth diagonal RAW square to one end of the neck band by weaving a connecting row of RAW picking up new As as the left and right bead of each RAW square(✴ **figure 7**).
28. Add a drop pendant to the center square stitch component on the bottom, and attach it to the checkerboard by sewing through the thread edges (**figure 8**).
29. Repeat to complete the other side of the necklace.

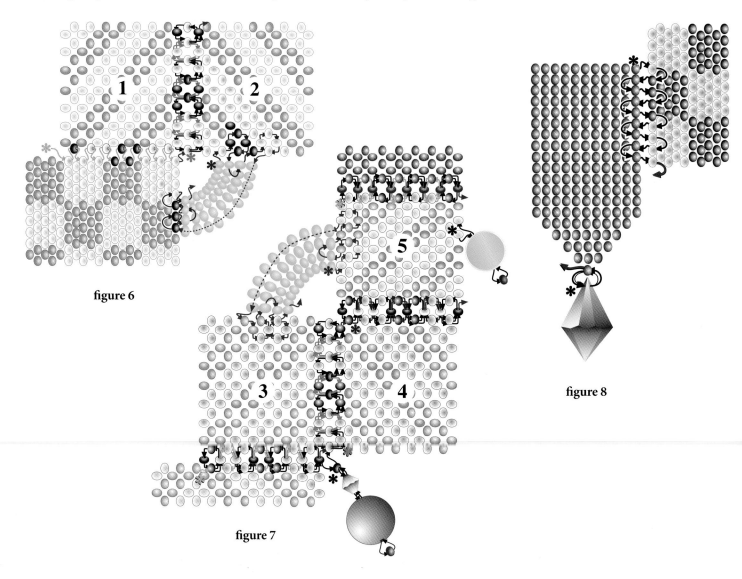

figure 6

figure 7

figure 8

June Huber started her beadweaving career in 2000 when she picked up her first beading project and was instantly hooked. Within months, she was creating her own designs. Since then, she has taught in the Houston area and at shows around the country. In 2007, she was invited to teach at the Bead Art Show in Yokohama, Japan. June's work has appeared in *Bead&Button* magazine, and she has had several pieces in juried shows, including *Bead&Button's* Bead Dreams. For more information, visit June's website, junipercreekdesigns.com.

Bugle Blocks Bracelet

stitch
ladder
level
intermediate

supplies
- **248** Japanese bugle beads size #1 (3 mm)
- **78** Japanese bugle beads size #3 (8 mm)
- **516** 15º seed beads
- **48** 8º seed beads
- **12** 4 mm fire-polished beads
- **2** ⁵⁄₁₆ in. (approx.) shank buttons
- Size A or B beading thread
- Size 12 beading needles

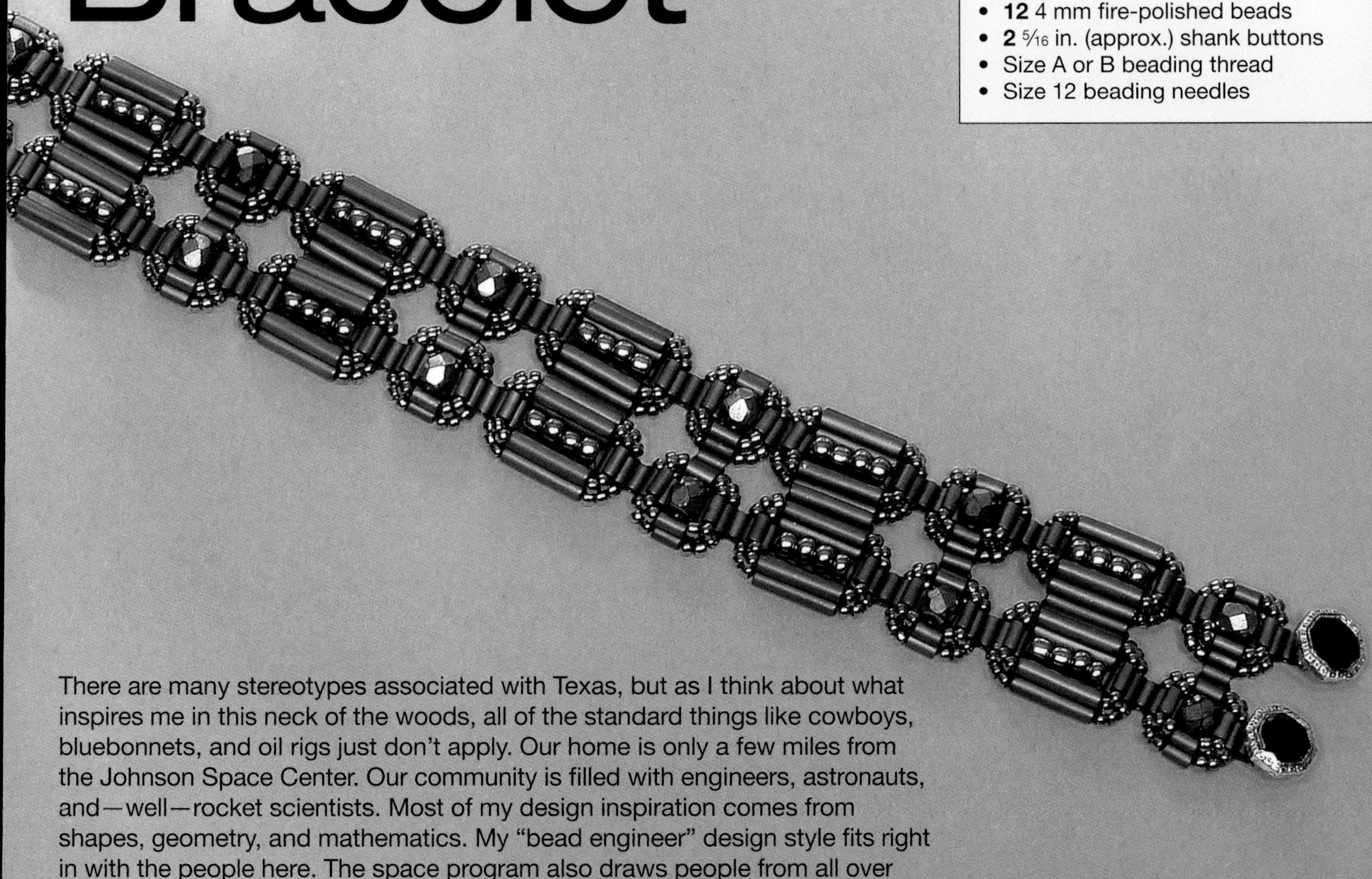

There are many stereotypes associated with Texas, but as I think about what inspires me in this neck of the woods, all of the standard things like cowboys, bluebonnets, and oil rigs just don't apply. Our home is only a few miles from the Johnson Space Center. Our community is filled with engineers, astronauts, and—well—rocket scientists. Most of my design inspiration comes from shapes, geometry, and mathematics. My "bead engineer" design style fits right in with the people here. The space program also draws people from all over the world. I've often been told that I don't sound like I'm from Houston. In my neighborhood, that could mean Russian, Swedish, Australian, German, Indian, and much more. I am inspired by the art and culture of faraway places, and have a lot of that here in my own backyard.

Building a square block

1. Thread a needle onto a comfortable length of thread and pick up two size #1 bugle beads, leaving a 6-in. tail. Circle through the first bugle again (ladder stitch). Sew around the circle a second time to anchor it (**figure 1**).

2. Pick up two more #1 bugles, and circle through the first to make a second pair. Slide the second pair of bugles against the first pair (**figure 2**).

3. Add two more pairs of #1 bugles in the same way. Sew through the first bugle where the thread tail is so that the four pairs are drawn into a square. There are four bugles that form an inner round and four bugles that form an outer round (**figure 3**).

4. Pick up a 15° seed bead and sew through the next bugle of the inner round. Repeat around the square, putting a 15° in each corner (**figure 4**).

Adding an accent bead

5. In the middle of the inner round, add a 4 mm fire-polished bead, as follows. With the thread, exit an inner round bugle, pick up the fire-polished bead and sew through the inner round bugle on the opposite side of the square. Sew through the fire-polished bead and sew through the first bugle again, following the thread path (**figure 5**).

6. Sew into the next inner round bugle. Make a U-turn by sewing through the outer round bugle next to the bugle the thread is exiting (**figure 6**).

7. Pick up a #1 bugle, and sew through the inner round bugle (**figure 6**). Go back through the new bugle and through the

outer round bugle. The new bugle should be anchored to the inner and outer bugles and sit neatly between them to form a triangular stack. Pick up three 15°s and sew through the next outer-round bugle (**figure 7**).

8. Repeat Step 7 around the block.

9. Make a U-turn through an upper round bugle next to where the thread is exiting. Pick up two 15°s and sew through the next upper bugle. Continue adding 15°s in each corner. This completes the first bugle block (**figure 8**).

Connecting the blocks

10. Make a U-turn and pick up an extra #1 bugle on one side of the block attached to the outer round bugle (used later to connect the second row of blocks). Sew through the three corner 15°s and the next

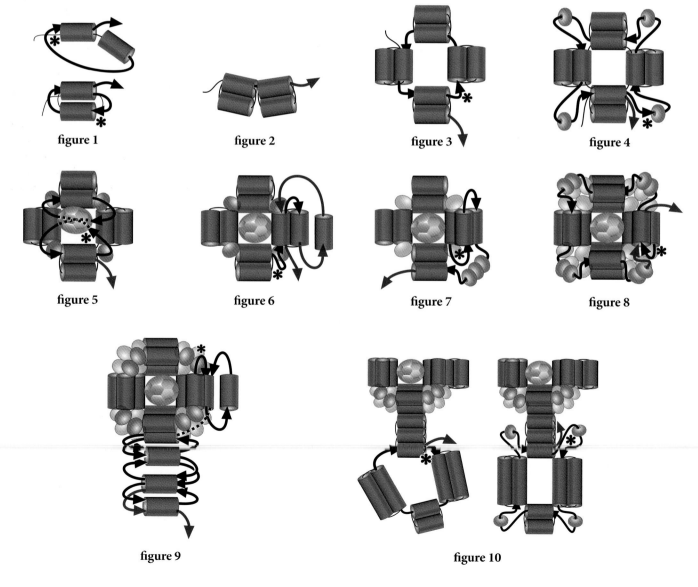

figure 1

figure 2

figure 3

figure 4

figure 5

figure 6

figure 7

figure 8

figure 9

figure 10

#1 bugle. Attach three new #1 bugles using ladder stitch (**figure 9**).

Building a rectangle block
11. Repeat Steps 2 and 3, using #3 bugles for the first and third pairs and #1 bugles for the second pair (**figure 10**).
12. Repeat Step 4.
13. For the center embellishment, pick up four 8°s and sew through the bugle on the opposite side of the rectangular opening. Sew back through the four 15°s, then sew through the first #1 bugle to complete the figure 8 of thread (**figure 11**). (Three 8°s may fill the center space as they can vary in size.)
14. Finish by following Steps 6–9 (**figures 6–8**), using #3 bugles on the longer sides and #1 bugles on the shorter sides. The thread path will be in the reverse direction.

15. Make a U-turn and add an extra #3 bugle along the same side as the first extra #1 bugle (**figure 12**).
16. Continue adding new blocks, alternating between squares and rectangles until the bracelet ends touch when wrapped around the wrist. The bracelet can end in a square or a rectangle.

Starting and ending thread: To end a thread or start a new one, use two side-by-side bugles on a finished block. Choose beads that won't be passed through again. Circle around between them two or three times. Don't force the needle through a bugle that is too full of thread. Start a new thread, leaving a 1-in. tail. Circle around through two bugles until the thread is secure, and trim the tail. Sew the thread into position to continue.

Building the second row of blocks
17. Use a new length of thread to make a square block (Steps 1–9).
18. Connect the new square block to the extra #1 bugle on the side of the existing block. Sew through the connecting blocks again for added strength (**figure 13**).
19. Continue adding new blocks in the second row, connect them to each other as before, and connect them to the extra #1 and #3 bugles on the first row (**figure 13**).

Making the button closure
20. Weave the thread to the #1 bugle at the end of the row. Use ladder stitch to add one #1 bugle. Sew around the thread path a second time for added strength (**figure 14**).
21. With the thread exiting the new bugle, pick up one 15°, the button shank, and one 15°. Pull the loop snug to make sure the two 15°s don't jump through the shank. Sew around this circle two to three times to secure, then sew through beads in the blocks to position the needle the same way on the second side. Repeat to attach the second button (**figure 14**). Anchor the thread securely, and cut.
22. On the opposite end, attach an extra #1 bugle and a loop of 15°s that will fit snugly around the button to each row of blocks Pass around each loop two to three times and sew into the extra bugle a second time for added strength (**figure 15**).

Beads vary in size. The two loops may contain a different amount of beads.

figure 11

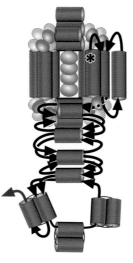

figure 12

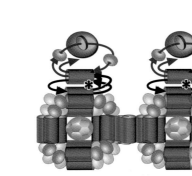

figure 13

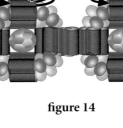

figure 14

figure 15

Nikia Angel has been beading obsessively since the 1980s. She spends her day surrounded by beautiful beads as she designs kits for her website, buythekit.com. She enjoys teaching at bead shows, bead stores, and informal kitchen gatherings.

Puerto de Luna Cristal Earrings

My inspiration for these simple drop earrings is a small town in east central New Mexico along the Pecos River called Puerto de Luna. The reddish bronze river banks are lined with dusty green olive and cypress trees. The town was originally settled by conquistadors on Coronado's trek north. The cross motif was prevalent in their clothing, and small carved ivory crosses have been found near the Pecos.

supplies
- 11º seed beads
  - **1 g A:** light aqua bronze lined
  - **1 g B:** heavy metal bronze AB
- **1 g** 15º seed beads heavy metal bronze AB
- **16** 3.5–4 mm side-drilled bronze freshwater pearls
- **30** 4 mm SWAROVSKI ELEMENTS bicones, olivine ABX2
- **2** 8 mm SWAROVSKI ELEMENTS bicones, olivine ABX2
- Pair of gold-filled earring wires
- Size 12 beading needles
- FireLine, 8-lb. test

Earring component 1

1. Thread a needle onto 3 ft. of thread. Pick up one A and one pearl four times. Go back through all the beads to make a circle. Pull tight, and tie a square knot. Sew through to the next A (**figure 1**).

2. Pick up two 15ºs, one A and two 15ºs. Skip the pearl, and sew through the next 11º. Continue adding two 15ºs, one A and two 15ºs all the way around (**figure 2**).

3. Exit through the next A of the beads just added. Pick up one 15º, one 4 mm crystal, one A, one 4 mm crystal, and one 15º. Skip five seed beads, and go through the A in the previous row. Continue all the way around (**figure 3**).

4. Exit the first crystal. Pick up three 15ºs and go through the next crystal to form a picot. Sew to the next crystal and continue to add picots all the way around. Exit the 11º of the previous row (**figure 4**).

5. To complete the back, pick up two 15ºs, one A and two 15ºs. Go though the next A of the same row (from Step 2). Continue all the way around (**figure 5**).

6. Come out through one of the As just added. Pick up one B. Continue all the way around, and pull tight. Reinforce by going back through all the beads in this row and the previous row (**figure 6**).

7. Sew over to one of the points through the second 15º on the picot.

8. Pick up one 15º, a 4 mm crystal, five 15ºs, the ear wire, and four 15ºs. Go back through the single 15º and the crystal. Pick up one 15º and go back through the 15º of the picot in the opposite direction (**figure 7**). Reinforce by going through all of the beads again. End the thread.

figure 1

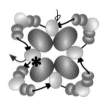

figure 2

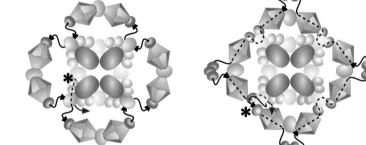

figure 3

figure 4

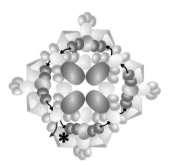

figure 5

figure 6

figure 7

Earring component 2

9. Repeat Steps 1–2.

10. Exit the next A of the beads just added.

11. Pick up one 15º, one 4 mm crystal, one A, one 4 mm crystal, and a 15º. Skip five seed beads (two 15ºs, one 11º, and two 15ºs of the previous row). Sew through the A and 15º (**figure 8**).

12. Pick up one 15º, one 4 mm crystal, and one 15º. Skip three beads (a 15º, 11º, and 15º). and go through the 15º and 11º of the previous row (**figure 8**).

13. Repeat Steps 11–12. This will bring you back to the start.

14. Sew through the 15º and crystal just added and pick up three 15ºs. Skip the 11º, and go through the next crystal. Sew through to the opposite end, and repeat the picot (**figure 9**).

15. Sew through to the opposite end, exit the second 15º of the picot.

16. Pick up one 15º, the 8 mm crystal, and four 15ºs. Skip three 15ºs and go back through one 15º and the crystal. Pick up one 15º and go through the second picot bead in the opposite direction (**figure 10**).

17. Complete the back, repeating Steps 5–6 (**figure 11**).

18. Sew through to the top of the component, and come out the second 15º of the picot. Pick up one 15º and go through the second 15º of the picot of the larger component. Pick up one 15º and go back through the picot of the smaller component in the opposite direction. Reinforce this connection (**figure 11**) and end the thread.

19. Make a second earring to match the first.

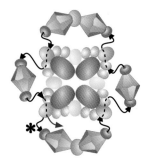

figure 8

figure 9

figure 10

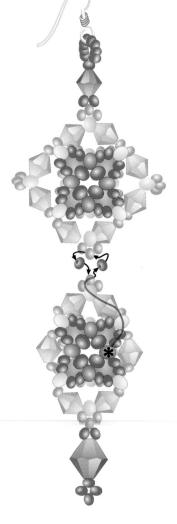

figure 11

Heidi Kummli's beadwork is an expression of herself, and her feelings for our Mother Earth and the creatures upon her. Through researching Native American beadwork techniques and trial and error, her work has continually evolved. Heidi started beading in 1975 and remembers making jewelry as a young child. She currently lives on 12 acres in Boulder, Colo., with her husband Gregg and their son Benjamin. Their home, totally off the grid, is powered by the sun and a back-up generator. Heidi has won numerous awards throughout her career. She hopes that through her work she can share the beauty that surrounds her. She is the coauthor of *The Art of Bead Embroidery* (Kalmbach 2007) with Sherry Serafini. Visit freespiritcollection.com to see more of Heidi's work.

Rocky Mountain Buzz Bracelet

I remember in the early 1990s when I got my first bag of Delicas: The colors and the consistency were a beader's dream come true and brought tears to my eyes. Because of their consistent shape and size they make loomwork easy and beautiful. This project is fun and shows a simple way to move your loomwork off the loom and attach it to whatever you like: barrette, necklace, leather, or in this case, a cuff bracelet. Feel free to change the pattern around; maybe you'd like a night sky with stars, or a beautiful sunrise. I used beads that I had available and you can too. The bee flew into my piece at the very end, but he can fly away and something else can land there, or maybe nothing at all. Make it your own with what you have.

stitch
loom

level
intermediate

supplies
- 11º cylinder beads (see chart for color suggestions)
- 15º seed beads
  10 g A: metallic bronze
  1 g B: yellow
  1 g C: orange
- 2 mm amber cabochon
- 4 mm opal cabochon
- Bee (Terra Cast)
- Bead loom, wood or other material
- Size 12 sharps needles
- Size 12 beading needles
- 2 pushpins
- ¾ in. masking tape
- Clear nail polish
- Aleen's™ Tacky Glue (thick preferably)
- Epoxy for cabochon
- Fabric lining
- Ultrasuede
- Small piece of poster board
- 1¼ in. wide metal cuff
- Size B thread, sand

Warping the loom

1. Place a pushpin on each end of a loom.
2. Tie the thread to the pushpin, leaving it attached to the spool. Tape a 2-in. tail onto the loom.

Put the spool on the floor so the thread comes off more easily.

3. Put the first warp thread through a groove at one end of the loom. Pull the warp thread through the groove on opposite side of the loom. Wrap the thread around the pushpin and into the next groove and across to the opposite end. Continue until there are 33 warp threads.
4. To tie off the thread, go around the pushpin four or five times, and tape the end to the loom. Make sure the threads are in the loom securely.

Weaving the pattern

5. Lay the beads on the right side of the loom and the pattern on the left.
6. Thread a beading needle with 4 ft. of thread. Attach this thread to the left warp thread leaving a 2-in. tail.

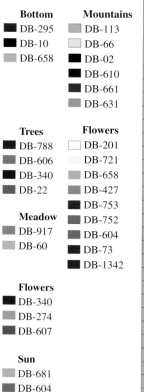

Bottom		Mountains	
▪	DB-295	▨	DB-113
▪	DB-10	▨	DB-66
▨	DB-658	▪	DB-02
		▪	DB-610
		▪	DB-661
		▨	DB-631

Trees		Flowers	
▪	DB-788	☐	DB-201
▨	DB-606	▨	DB-721
▪	DB-340	▨	DB-658
▨	DB-22	▨	DB-427
		▪	DB-753
Meadow		▨	DB-752
▨	DB-917	▨	DB-604
▨	DB-60	▪	DB-73
		▪	DB-1342

Flowers	
▪	DB-340
▨	DB-274
▪	DB-607

Sun	
▨	DB-681
▨	DB-604

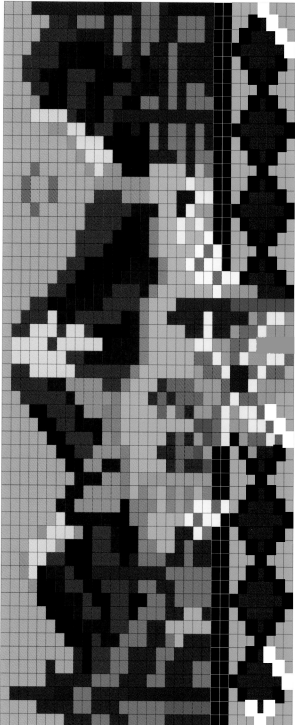

figure 1

7. Pick up 32 cylinder beads as specified in the pattern. Pull them all the way down to the knot. Push all the beads up between the warp threads with your hand. The weaving thread always goes under the warp threads when you are adding beads (**figure 1**).
8. Once the last bead is in place, take the needle around the far right warp thread to the top of the threads and back through the beads. For the first row, sew back through each bead individually. Use your left index finger to push the beads up while your right hand controls the needle.
9. Pull the weaving thread as tight as possible. The first row will not stay tight until the second row is added.

10. Repeat Steps 7–9 for Row 2 using the colors indicated in the pattern. Try to keep the beads in straight rows, fairly tight.

11. Continue the pattern. To start a new thread, tie a knot on the left warp thread following Step 6. To end a thread, tie a knot on the left warp. Go back through a row of beads to hide the thread, and trim.

Finishing the woven piece

12. Once the loomwork is completed, seal the knots and warp threads next to the beads with clear nail polish and let dry.

13. On each side of the loomwork, tape the warp threads to secure. (The tape will be hidden under the back of the loom-work later.) Leave a little space between the loomwork and the tape or it will show when folded under.

14. Pull the pushpins out of the loom and take the beadwork off the loom. Cut the warp threads close to the tape, leaving a small amount of tape on the warp threads so they can be easily thrown away.

15. Fold the tape behind the loomwork.

16. Cut a piece of fabric lining slightly smaller than the loomed piece. Glue the lining to the loomed piece using Tacky Glue.

17. After gluing, lay the beadwork under something flat and heavy, such as a cutting board or book, for 15 minutes. This helps keep the piece nice and flat while drying.

Adding the cabochons

18. Using epoxy, glue the amber cabochon to the sun and the opal cabochon to the flower's center. Put a dab of glue on the loomwork, and work it into the cylinder beads where each cabochon will sit. Put a dab of glue on each cabochon.

19. Place the cabochons in position and let the glue set for the manufacturer's recommended time.

20. Thread 2 ft. of thread on a sharp needle and knot the thread. Sew up through the loomwork next to the opal cabochon.

21. Pick up four As and lay them flat against the cabochon. Backstitch using four beads at a time around the cabochon. Go through all the 15ºs one more time (**figure 2**).

22. Use Bs to accent the flower. Exit a 15º on the backstitched row, pick up Bs and sew through the next 15º.

23. Repeat Steps 20–21 using Cs to accent the amber cabochon.

24. Position the bee near the flower, and stitch it in place.

Finishing the bracelet

25. Cut a 1½ x 6 in. pattern from poster board. Using a ruler and marker, draw lines approximately ¼ in. larger than the pattern on the Ultrasuede. Make sure the marks are on the back of the Ul-trasuede. Cut out the Ultrasuede. This piece will be glued inside the metal cuff.

26. Cut two 2 x 1½ in. pieces of Ultrasuede. These will be used for the top of the cuff next to the loomwork.

27. Using Tacky Glue, glue the large piece of Ultrasuede to the inside of the metal cuff. Spread the glue with a toothpick. Center the Ultrasuede on the cuff and smooth it down. Trim the ends of the Ultrasuede ¼ in. larger than the round edges of the cuff.

28. Glue the two Ultrasuede end tabs on to the front of the metal cuff. Apply Tacky

Glue to the back of the Ultrasuede and glue it down flatly.

29. Apply Tacky Glue to the back of the loomwork, and center it on the cuff. Use your fingers to smooth out the loomwork.

30. Let it dry about 20 minutes. Clothespins work well to hold the piece in place while it dries.

Edge the bracelet

31. Thread a sharps needle with 2 ft. of thread, and knot the end. Bring the knot between the loomwork and the backing. Sew down through the bottom Ultrasuede about 1⁄16 in. from the edge.

32. Start the edge at any corner by sewing up through the warp thread. Pick up four As and sew through the Ultrasuede about 1⁄8 in. from where you started, and go back through the last bead added. Pull the beads snug (**figure 3**).

33. Continue Step 32 all along the edge, grabbing the warp threads in each edge stitch.

34. At the ends of the bracelet, pick up four As, go under the warp thread between every third bead, and back through the last bead added (✳ **figure 3**).

35. Repeat the edge on the Ultrasuede tabs on each end.

36. Once the piece is edged, secure the thread in the backing. Use a damp Q-tip to clean excess glue from the Ultrasuede.

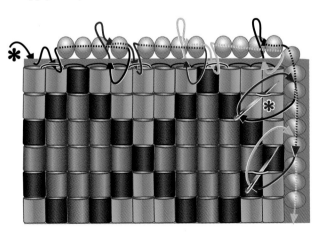

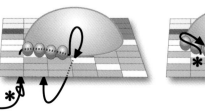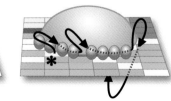

figure 2

figure 3

Scarlett Lanson made her big debut to the beading community when she nabbed back-to-back Swarovski Design Contest wins at age 17. From there, she became a contributing editor for a major beading magazine writing a regular column, *Scarlett's Style*. She sells her wares professionally through trunk shows and produces an exclusive line of jewelry for the destination spa, Enchantment Resort. Now 20, she is most proud of creating and organizing a reoccurring global beading contest, "Use the Muse," held on her website, thebeadersmuse.com.

Sedona Sunset Earrings

From my studio retreat in Sedona, Ariz., I am surrounded by gorgeous red rock views and am honored to live in such a creative mecca. Arizona is known for its natural beauty and has become a place to which people flock to heal their spirits and reclaim their inner artist. When the pressures and chaos of running my own business get to me, I can take my dogs out for a stroll, soak in the scenery, and be reminded by my muse why I do what I do. Every time, all it takes is a connection with the Arizona earth to rekindle my creative energy.

stitch and technique
circular brick, circular peyote, basic wirework

level
intermediate

supplies
- 8º seed beads, **2 g** each of
  A: matte brown
  B: metallic plum iris
  C: matte metallic plum iris
  D: metallic rust
- 11º seed beads
  3 g E: metallic rust
  2 g F: matte metallic raku purple
  2 g G: matte brown
  1 g H: dark metallic purple
- 15º seed beads
  1 g I: matte brown
  1 g J: light transparent metallic bronze
  1 g K: 24kt gold iris
  1 g L: dark metallic purple
  1 g M: matte metallic raku purple
- 4 mm SWAROVSKI ELEMENTS pearls
  10 bordeaux
  4 gold
  2 copper
  2 platinum
- 3 ft. 20-gauge copper wire
- Pair of copper earring wires
- **16** 5 mm open oval copper jump rings
- FireLine, 6-lb. test, smoke
- Size 12 beading needles
- ½ in. wide bead tube and tapered bottleneck for shaping wire
- Wire cutters
- Roundnose pliers
- Flatnose pliers

Creating the disks

Follow the color key for the individual ombré color patterns for each disk. Each earring consists of nine disks.

1. Thread a needle onto 2 ft. of thread, leaving a 6-in. tail. Each disk will have four rounds.

Round One: Pick up one pearl and five 11ºs. Knot the working thread and tail. Pull the knot so it is concealed within the pearl. Pick up five 11ºs. Sew though the pearl and the 11ºs just added. Pick up one 11º and sew through the next five 11ºs around the pearl. Pick up one 11º and sew through the next two 11ºs to form a complete ring around the pearl (**figure 1**).

Round Two: Begin circular brick stitch by picking up one 11º, one 15º, and one 11º to form a picot. Stitch the picot between the next two 11ºs on the ring. Continue to pick up one 15º and one 11º to form picots all the way around. For the twelfth and last stitch in the row, pick up only one 15º, and connect it to the first 11º of this round (**figure 2**).

Round Three: With the thread exiting the top of the next picot, pick up one 8º and peyote stitch into the next 15º. Continue all the way around. Step up to begin the next round (**figure 3**).

Round Four: Pick up one 15º, one 11º, and one 15º and peyote stitch into the next 8º in the previous row. Continue all the way around (**figure 4**).

Important: While stitching, pull the 11º in each picot to make it jut out. The 15ºs should be pushing the 11ºs out at an angle. Otherwise the piece will warp.

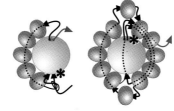

figure 1

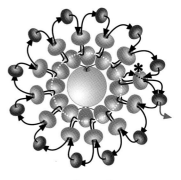

figure 2

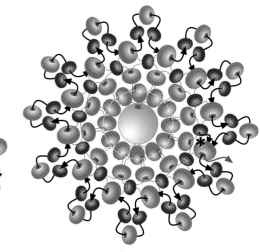

figure 3

figure 4

2. Loop: Position the thread to exit the top 11º of a picot. See the Color Key below for disks to determine the loop placement for each disk. Pick up five 15ºs. Pass through the original 11º again to form a ring. Reinforce it twice, tying several knots between the beads. Work the remaining thread into the last round of beads, secure, and trim the excess thread (**figure 5**).

Color key for disks

Disk 1: copper pearl
Round 1: Es
Round 2: Es, Is
Round 3: Ds
Round 4: Is, Es
Loop: Is
Placement: anywhere on the outside of the disk

Disks 2 and 3: bordeaux pearl
Round 1: Es
Round 2: Es, Is
Round 3: stitches 1–4 Ds, stitches 5–12 Bs
Round 4: J s, Es
Loop: Is
Placement: off the top 11º of the picot between the second and third Ds of Round 3

Disks 4 and 6: bordeaux pearl
Round 1: G
Round 2: Gs, Ms
Round 3: stitches 1–4 Bs, stitches 5–12 Cs
Round 4: stitches 1–6 and 10–12 Js and Es, stitches 7–9 Ks and Es.
Loop: Is
Placement: off the top 11º of the picot between the second and third Bs of Round 3

Disk 5: bordeaux pearl
Round 1: Es
Round 2: Es, Ms
Round 3: stitches 1–4 Bs, stitches 5–12 Cs
Round 4: stitches 1–6 and 10-12 Js and Es, stitches 7–9 Ks and Es
Loop: Ks
Placement: off the top 11º of the picot between the second and third Bs of Round 3

Disks 7 and 8: gold pearl
Round 1: Fs
Round 2: Fs, Ks
Round 3: stitches 1–8 As, stitches 9–12 Cs
Round 4: stitches 1–7 Ks and Hs, stitches 8–12 Ls and Hs
Loop: Ks
Placement: off the top 11º of the picot between the fourth and fifth As of Round 3

Disk 9: platinum pearl
Round 1: Fs
Round 2: Fs, Ks
Round 3: stitches 1–8 As, stitches 9–12 Cs
Round 4: Ls and Hs
Loop: Ks
Placement: off the top 11º of the 11º picot between the fourth and fifth As of Round 3

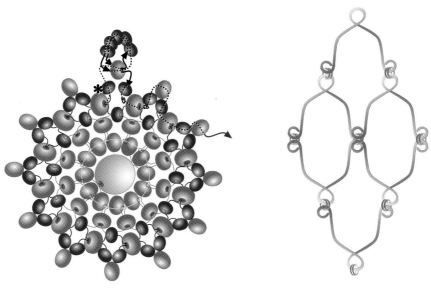

figure 5   figure 6

Forming the framework

3. Create a slight coil in the wire by taking it off a spool, or by wrapping it around a 1½ in. diameter bottle neck. Cut six 2-in. pieces (**figure 6**).

4. Grasp a piece of wire in the middle with roundnose pliers. Carefully pull one end down and around the pliers jaw. Do not pull out. Keep the U shape established by the wire. Carefully pull the other end down and around so the wire resembles an upside down "U" with a loop at the top where the pliers are gripping it (**figure 6**).

5. Pick up the plastic tube. Place the open ends of the "U" around the top of the plastic tube. Press the sides of the wire against it gently to reinforce the rounded shape. Smooth out any kinks.

6. On one end, carefully roll the wire outwards with roundnose pliers to create a single loop. Repeat on the other end. Forming the loop creates the bell shape of the finding.

7. Repeat with the remaining cut wires to form six bell-shaped findings.

Assembling the earring

8. Assemble the disks according to the pattern (**figure 7**). Connect the bottom loop of one frame with the top loop of another using jump rings. Repeat to connect all the frames. At the center, use one jump ring to connect two pairs of overlapping loops. Leave the jump rings open as you work.

9. Layer the beaded disks onto the frames and the open jump rings. Close the jump rings.

> Close the jump rings as tightly as possible so that the wire won't show through.

10. Attach the bottom of the last bell finding with a jump ring and pick up the loop of disk 9. Attach the earring wire to the top loop of the first bell.

11. Make a second earring to match the first.

figure 7

Sherri Haab is a bestselling craft author with over 25 published books to her credit. She is a certified metal clay instructor, leading numerous craft and jewelry-making workshops internationally. She also develops new craft products and provides consulting services for the craft industry. Sherri has released two DVDs (*Metal Clay* and *Resin*) and has appeared on several local and national television and radio programs. She resides in Springville, Utah, with her husband Dan, who engineers products for Sherri Haab Designs. They have three children who also help with various projects ranging from web design to video production. Visit her website, sherrihaab.com.

Beaded Bee Bracelet

Utah is known as the beehive state. Mormon pioneers, including a few of my ancestors, braved harsh conditions to settle in the Rocky Mountains in the mid 1800s. They were known for their perseverance and hard work. The honeybee came to represent the industry and cooperation of the people of Utah and became the state's symbol. I value the work ethic, determination, and integrity passed down through my family that the bees represent. I also love bee-themed illustrations and design in general. I often include bee designs in my jewelry.

stitch
macramé
level
intermediate

supplies

- 12 yds. C-Lon thread cord (#18 nylon) cut into **8** 1½-yd. pieces (janesfiberandbeads.com)
- Centerpiece silver bee charm with 3 or 4 holes on each side (sherrihaabdesigns.com)
- **10** or more semiprecious stone beads, **4** larger (10 mm) and **6** smaller (6–7 mm)
- **60–80** 11º metal silver-plated seed beads
- Magnetic clasp or tube slide clasp
- Foamcore or clipboard
- Binder clips
- **2** T-pins
- Thread Zapper

Knotting the bracelet

1. Fold two cords in half and bring the middles through the center hole of the charm. Pull the cord ends through the loop to form a lark's head knot. Pull the knot tight and make sure the ends are even.

2. Attach single cords to the remaining holes with lark's head knots, so there are eight cord ends in total.

3. Secure the piece on a clipboard or foamcore using binder clips. Number the cords from left to right (1–8).

4. Bring Cord 1 across the other cords as shown (**figure 1**). Tie a double half-hitch knot over Cord 1 with each cord (2–8), moving left to right (**figure 2**).

5. Bring Cord 1 back across the cords to the left and secure with a T-pin.

Tie a second row of double half-hitch knots as before (**figure 3**).

6. Slide a silver bead onto Cord 2. Tie a square knot under the bead using Cords 1 and 3, using Cord 2 as the core cord. Slide a silver bead on Cord 7. Tie a square knot under the bead using Cords 6 and 8 with Cord 7 as the core (**figure 4**).

7. Re-number the cords. Slide one silver bead onto the two middle cords (Cords 4 and 5). Tie a square knot under the bead using Cords 3 and 6 with Cords 4 and 5 as the core. There are three square knots across the row (**figure 5**).

8. Slide a small semiprecious stone onto Cord 4. Tie a square knot under the stone with Cords 3 and 5, with 4 as the core (**figure 6**).

figure 1

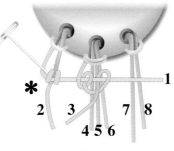

figure 2

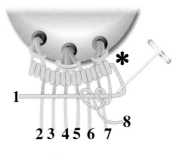

figure 3

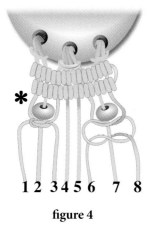

figure 4

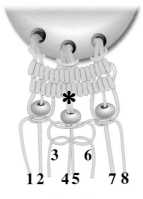

figure 5

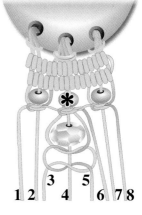

figure 6

9. Tie a square knot with Cords 5 and 7 over Cord 6. Adjust the tension of the cords so that the square knot forms next to the square knot under the bead from the last step (**figure 7**).

10. Slide two silver beads onto Cord 1 and two silver beads onto Cord 8. Tie a square knot with Cords 1 and 3 over core 2, and Cords 6 and 8 over core 7. There will be four square knots in the row (**figure 8**).

11. Slide one large semiprecious stone bead over Cords 4 and 5 close to the knots. Tie a square knot under the bead with Cords 3 and 6 (**figure 9**).

12. Tie a lark's head knot with Cord 7 over Cord 8 (**figure 10**).

13. Slide a silver bead onto Cord 7 and tie a lark's head knot under the bead. Continue to tie a sennit (series) of knots alternating with silver beads until you have three beads total. End with a knot (**figure 10**).

14. Repeat steps 12–13 on the left side of the large bead (**figure 10**).

15. Tie a square knot on the left side with Cords 1 and 3 over Cord 2. Tie a square knot on the right side with Cords 6 and 8 over Cord 7. There are now three square knots in the row (**figure 11**).

16. Slide another small semiprecious stone onto Cord 5. Tie a square knot under the stone with Cords 4 and 6. Tighten the cords so the square knot forms next to the square knot under the bead (**figure 12**).

17. Tie a square knot with Cords 2 and 4 over Cord 3 (**figure 12**).

18. Tie two more square knots in this row: Cords 6 and 8 over Cord 7 and Cords 1 and 3 over Cord 2.

19. Repeat Steps 11–15.

20. Repeat Steps 8–10.

21. Complete the knotted sequence with a row of three silver beads followed by three square knots tied under each (Steps 6–7).

22. Tie two rows of double half-hitch knots, as at the start.

23. Repeat Steps 1–21 on the other side of the focal bead.

24. Tie all eight cords on one end through the loop of half the clasp and pull tightly. Repeat with the other clasp half on the other end of the bracelet.

25. Finish the ends by knotting two cords together at a time with an overhand knot to form four ends on each side of the bracelet. Clip the cord ends close to the knots and melt them with a Thread Zapper to finish.

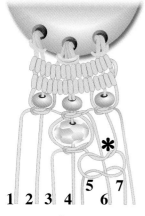

figure 7

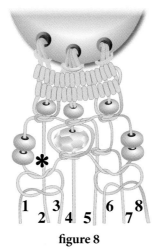

figure 8

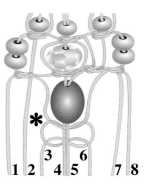

figure 9

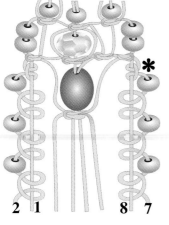

figure 10

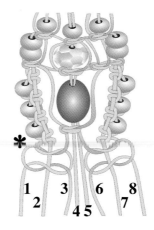

figure 11

figure 12

Susan Barrett wandered into a bead store looking for seed beads for a cross stitch project 10 years ago, and has been beading ever since. She enjoys all beadweaving stitches. She began teaching locally in 2000 and branched out nationally in 2008. Her greatest joy is introducing new students to the pleasure and satisfaction of creating their own works of art. Learn more about Susan's work at beadgoddessdesigns.com.

Nevada Flowers & Buds

Living in southern Nevada for the past 12 years has given me a great appreciation for the state I now call home. While most people associate Nevada with gambling, it also boasts first-class entertainment, museums, and outdoor activities such as bike riding, hiking, and camping. During the summer you can spend the day at Lake Mead and in the winter you can ski on Mt. Charleston.

stitch
right-angle weave
level
all levels

supplies
- **3 g** 11º seed beads, palladium plated
- **200** 4 mm Czech fire-polished beads, silver-lined
- 4 mm SWAROVSKI ELEMENTS bicones
    - **56 A:** sun
    - **56 B:** light emerald
    - **28 C:** hyacinth
    - **28 D:** rose
- **43** anti-nickel rhodium plated SWAROVSKI ELEMENTS sliders, fuchsia
- 6 mm two-strand bar clasp
- **4** 8 mm jump rings
- Microcystalline wax
- Size 10 or 12 beading needles
- FireLine, 8-lb.test
- Glue, GS-Hypo cement or similar
- Chainnose pliers

Larger wrists may need additional beads.

Bracelet base
1. Thread a needle onto 2 yds. of thread and wax it.

2. Pick up four fire-polished beads, leaving a 6-in. tail. Sew through all four beads again in the same direction, and knot the thread. Sew through the first two fire-polished beads again (**figure 1**).

3. Pick up three fire-polished beads, and go through the bead your thread is exiting. Pick up three more beads and repeat. Stitch three squares of right-angle weave (RAW) with the fire-polished beads. There should be four fire-polished beads in each square. Pull snug to position the beads. This is the first row (**figure 2**).

4. Position the needle to begin the second row of RAW as shown (**figure 2**).

5. Continue stitching rows of RAW until you reach the desired length of the bracelet, minus the measurement needed for the clasp (approximately ½–¾ in.).

Embellishing the base
6. Thread a needle onto 2 yds. of conditioned thread. Anchor the thread at either end of the bracelet base by tying half-hitch knots.

7. Sew through to the left square of the first row, exiting through the top of the fire-polished bead on the upper left edge.

8. Pick up one A, one 11º seed bead and one A. Sew the thread through the fire-polished bead on the opposite side from bottom to top (**figure 3**).

9. Pick up one A. Sew through the 11º from Step 8 (**figure 3**).

10. Pick up one A. Sew through the fire-polished bead on the left from bottom to top. Sew through to the center square (**figure 4**).

11. Pick up a slider, passing through the holes from lower right to upper left. Sew through the fire-polished bead at the top of this square, from left to right. Sew through the upper right and lower left holes of the slider (**figure 5**).

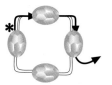

figure 1

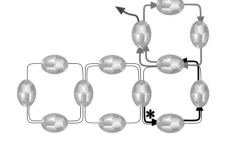

figure 2

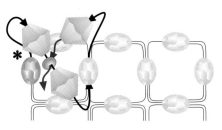

figure 3

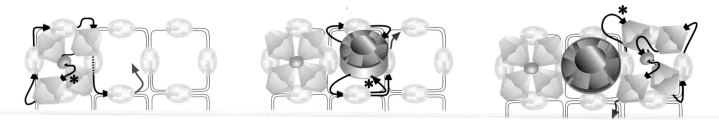

figure 4

figure 5

figure 6

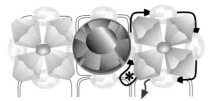

figure 7

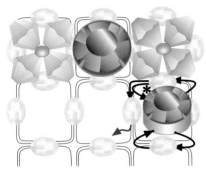

figure 8

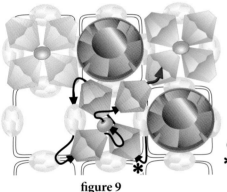

figure 9

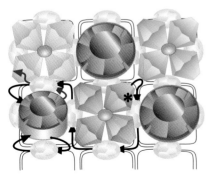

figure 10

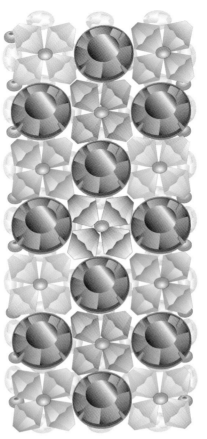

figure 11

figure 12

12. Repeat the thread paths in Step 11 to reinforce the slider. Exit the fire-polished bead on the right.

13. With the needle exiting the top of the fire-polished bead of the last square of the row, repeat Steps 8–10 with Bs (**figure 6**).

14. Come out the left side of the top fire-polished in row 2 (**figure 7**). Pick up a slider on the needle, passing through the holes from upper left to lower right (**figure 8**).

15. Sew through the fire-polished bead at the bottom of this square from right to left. Sew through the lower left and upper right holes of the slider. Reinforce again.

16. Pick up one C, one 11° and one C. Follow the thread path in the diagram to attach it to the fire-polished beads. Attach the remainder of the bicones as indicated (**figures 9 and 10**). Attach a slider as in Step 15 (**figure 10**).

17. Use the chart to determine color placement of the bicones. Continue alternating the pattern with 11°s and sliders as shown until reaching the end. Alternate the color of the center bicones between C and D (**figure 11**).

18. Add one 11° between each fire-polished bead on both of the long edges. Secure the thread with half-hitch knots.

Attaching the clasp

19. Thread a needle onto 2 yds. of thread. Secure it in the beadwork with half-hitch knots. Exit the fire-polished beads along the short edge of the bracelet.

20. Insert a jump ring into the next space between the fire-polished bead and sew through the jump ring and the next fire-polished bead. Insert a jump ring into the next space and sew through the jump ring and the last fire-polished bead along the edge (**figure 12**).

21. Sew through the next horizontal row and back to the other side. Reinforce the jump rings several times. Secure the thread in the beadwork with half-hitch knots.

22. Use chainnose pliers to open the jump rings, and attach clasp. Close the jump rings and place a dot of glue over the opening to seal them.

23. Repeat Steps 19–22 on the opposite side.

Jeanette Shanigan's passion for beads began in the 1960s with love beads and macramé. She has written nearly a dozen beadwork books and many articles for bead magazines. Jeanette teaches at many shows including Embellishment, *Bead&Button*, Bead Expo, and BeadFest, as well as two workshops in Ireland for Beadventures. Summer days find Jeanette in Alaskan waters working as a cruise-ship travel guide. During the long Alaskan winters, she is hard at work on bead quilts to raise money for breast cancer research or creating more designs for additional beadwork books and kits. Visit her website, shanigansbeadshenanigans.com, or e-mail jshanigan@hotmail.com.

Moose Forget-Me-Not Pin

stitch
brick
level
beginner

supplies
- 11º round seed beads, small quantities of brown, tan, black, green, blue, yellow
- Nymo D thread
- Size 12 beading needles
- 1 in. pinback
- Quick Grip Glue or similar product

Alaska is one of the top 10 travel destinations in the world, as evidenced by the million-and-a-half visitors annually. It's a wild, remote place chock full of stunning mountain vistas, hundreds of thousands of glistening blue glaciers, three million lakes, and 3,000 rivers—not to mention many, many varieties of wild critters. Life in the "last frontier" is always an adventure and a bit of a challenge; one never knows what to expect from Mother Nature. She routinely presents colorful, dancing Northern Lights, exploding volcanoes, 5,000 earthquakes annually, and a wide range of weather possibilities. All of this, in addition to the 11 unique cultures of Alaska's indigenous people, continually inspire and motivate me to bead Alaska. This pin features one of Alaska's iconic wild critters, the moose. Prominently displayed in the antlers are forget-me-nots, the Alaska state flower.

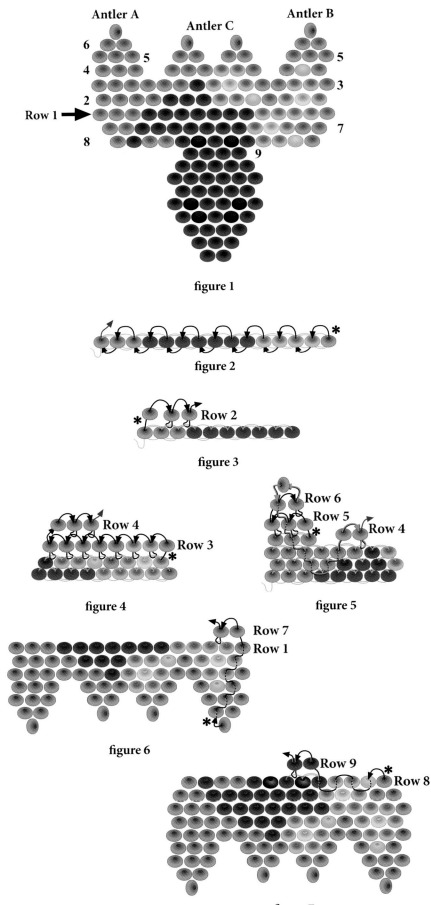

Antler A
Antler C
Antler B

6
5
4
Row 1 →
2
8
3
7
9

figure 1

figure 2

Row 2

figure 3

Row 4
Row 3

Row 6
Row 5
Row 4

figure 4

figure 5

Row 7
Row 1

figure 6

Row 9
Row 8

figure 7

1. Starting at Row 1, stitch a bead ladder 15 beads wide. For this and all subsequent rows, stitch the beads as indicated in the pattern (**figure 1**).

2. Reinforce the ladder row by sewing back through all of the beads (**figure 2**).

3. Working the top of the pattern, brick stitch to the top of the antlers. Rows 2, 4 and 6 begin with a regular start. Rows 3 and 5 begin with an increase brick stitch start (**figure 3**). Brick stitch three beads for Row 4 and complete Antler A by stitching Rows 5 and 6. The bead point of the antler is looped on top of Row 6 (**figures 4, 5**).

4. After stitching the point, sew through the beads to get the needle in position to stitch the rest of Row 4 (**figure 5**).

5. Stitch the first three beads of Row 5, and complete Antler B. The bead point is looped on top of Row 6.

6. Sew through the beadwork, and complete Antler C. The bead points of the antlers are looped on top of Row 5.

7. Sew through the beadwork to the beginning of Row 1. Turn the piece upside-down, and stitch Rows 7 and 8, beginning with a regular brick stitch start and noting the color pattern (**figure 6**).

8. Sew through the beadwork to stitch Row 9 of the snout. Begin Row 9 with a regular brick stitch start (**figure 7**). Rows 10, 12, 14, 15, 16, and 17 begin with regular brick stitch start. Rows 11 and 13 begin with an increase brick stitch start (**figure 8**).

9. When the moose is completed, secure the threads, and trim. Glue the pinback across the antlers at Row 1 on the back of the beadwork. Allow it to dry completely before wearing.

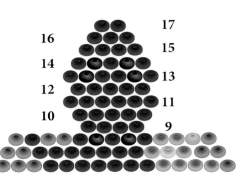

16
17
14
15
12
13
10
11
9

figure 8

Beverly Ash Gilbert travels around the country teaching classes and workshops that focus on free-form beadweaving and working with color. She created *Beverly's Bead Soup Collection* with over 50 different colorways and has written two books: *Eye For Color: Interchangeable Templates and Color Wheel System* and *Beaded Colorways: Creating Freeform Beadweaving Projects and Palettes* (Northlight Books 2008). Contact Beverly on her website, gilbertdesigns.net and follow along with her day-to-day musings and inspirations on her blog, beverlygilbert.blogspot.com.

Sea Glass Necklace

The vast waterways of Puget Sound wind through islands and deep green forests of northwest Washington. I grew up surrounded by the lush greens and blues of water, mountains, and trees and feel at home listening to bird song and lapping waves. Beaches are everywhere, full of sea glass, driftwood, shells, and old metal bits from fishing boats—a beachcomber's paradise. Earthy, organic, outdoorsy, natural—these elements are ingrained in native Washingtonians and weave their way into my bead soups and free-form beadwork. In this necklace, colors flow together as organic strands of beads and gems wind in and around antiqued metal and sea glass found after a day at the beach.

stitch
free-form netting
level
all levels

supplies

- **5–10** pieces sea glass any shape or size (triangular pieces are easiest to surround)
- 24-gauge sheet metal, plain, etched, or colorized (the metal here was altered with balsamic vinegar, salt, and heat)
- **60–120 g** seed bead soup in colors to complement sea glass: sizes 15º, 11º, 8º, 6º, 5º; shapes such as cylinder, hex-cut, triangle, charlotte, bugle, magatama; and finishes like matte, shiny, AB, and lined (Beverly's Bead Soup Collection at gilbertdesigns.net)
- Handful of 2–10 mm accent beads: gems, pearls, shells, old coins, etc.
- **1–2** size 3 sew-on snaps
- Favorite beading thread
- Size 12 beading needles
- Beeswax
- Bead mat, tray, or extra mat for bead soup
- Metal shears (jewelry grade)
- Metal file
- Large roundnose pliers or mandrel

Free-form beadweaving is full of movement and life. This list is a guide; the quantities, sizes, and beads you choose may evolve as your project takes shape.

Making the metal pieces

1. Using metal shears, cut strips, squares, or rectangles out of sheet metal. Make the shapes compatible in size to the sea glass.
2. File the edges with a metal file, removing all burs, sharp corners, and rough edges. Carefully run fingers along the edges to verify the smoothness.
3. Using roundnose pliers or other mandrel, bend and contort the metal pieces to create asymmetrical waves **(figure 1)**.

Planning the necklace

4. Lay out the sea glass and metal pieces on the bead mat. Determine the total length based on size and shape of glass and metal elements and the fit around the neck. Pour the bead soup around the elements to visualize the look of the piece. Adjust the components to make a pleasing design. This is a guideline. Changes can be made as the work develops.

Beginning the necklace

5. Thread a needle onto a comfortable length of thread, doubled and waxed. Attach a stop bead, leaving a 4-in. tail.
6. Pick up a random mix of seed beads (bead soup) to the length measured in Step 4 plus approximately 5–6 in. Turn the corner by sewing back into the eighth bead (approximately) from the end to create a smooth loop **(figure 2)**.

7. Pick up a random number of seed beads and sew into a bead from the first row so the length of beads added is equal to the length of beads skipped. Adjust the tension to prevent exposed thread **(figure 3)**.

> Avoid using accent beads on the first few rows since they may be hidden. Use accent beads after the sea glass and metal are enclosed to fill in the necklace.

8. Repeat Step 7 to end the first row, making sure stitches are varied in length **(figure 3)**. Remove excess beads and the stop bead at the end. Adjust the tension, and tie half-hitch knots to secure the beads. Don't cut the thread.
9. Turn the corners by picking up approximately five seed beads, and sewing any bead from the last group of beads added on the second row. Adjust the number of beads picked up and the number of beads skipped so that the loops are pleasing and there are no exposed threads **(figure 4)**.
10. Follow Step 7 to the end of the row, making a seed bead base of three rows. Turn the corner as in Step 9. End and start new lengths of thread as needed. Weave the ends into the beadwork in a full circle before cutting. Thread a needle onto the tail, and sew it into the beadwork in the same manner.

figure 1

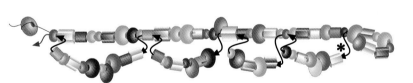

figure 3

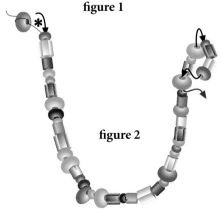

figure 2

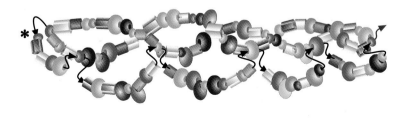

figure 4

Enclosing the sea glass

11. Place the seed bead base on top or underneath the sea glass or tuck the glass into an open loop of beadwork to obtain a pleasing look. Hold the glass in place.

12. Sew through the beadwork until the needle exits at one edge of the glass. Pick up enough seed beads to stretch from the edge across the glass to the seed bead base on the opposite edge. Sew into the base on the second edge to form a strand around the glass (**figure 5**).

13. Sew in a circle through the beadwork until the needle is facing the new strand. Build up the strand with free-form stitches about one to five beads in length.

14. Add and build up new strands by stitching between the seed bead base and the strand added in Step 12. Surround the glass on all sides.

15. Add webs between the strands to increase tension, secure strands onto glass, and provide an organic feel to the piece. When the glass is secure, and there are no holes bigger than the glass, it is complete.

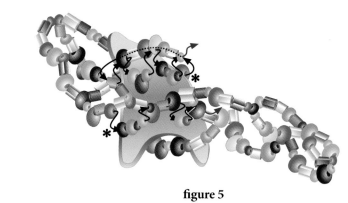

figure 5

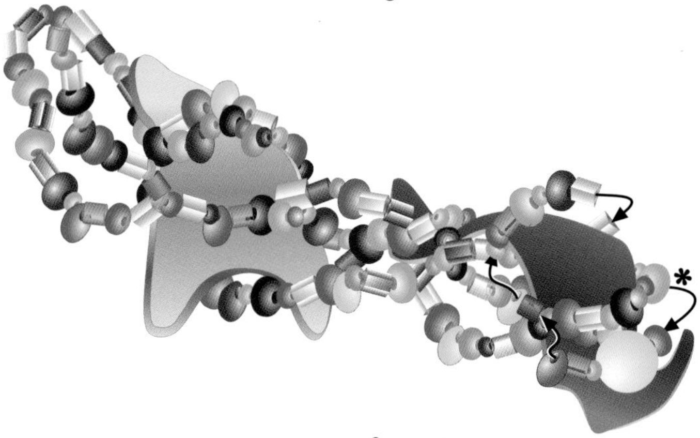

Enclosing the metal

16. Wrap the seed bead base around the metal (patina side up), coaxing it into the ridges and valleys. Add and build up strands and webs following Steps 12–15, until the metal is secure (**figure 6**).

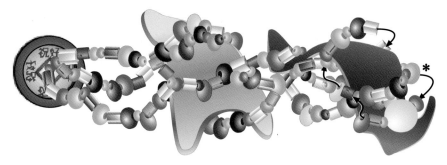

figure 6

> To add more length to the base strand, weave through the beadwork until the needle exits one end. Pick up one length of seed beads as in Step 6, then turn the corner and build up the seed bead base following Steps 7–8.

Filling in the necklace

17. Repeat Steps 11–16, alternating pieces of sea glass and metal.

18. Continue enclosing pieces of sea glass and metal until the necklace is full. Add new strands of beads to enhance the organic flow. Add accent gems as desired.

19. Add strands of seed beads to both ends of the necklace, which will be the base for the clasp. A clasp also can be created by netting a coin (**figure 7**).

20. Sew closure snaps into the beadwork on the back for both sides of the clasp (**figure 8**).

figure 7

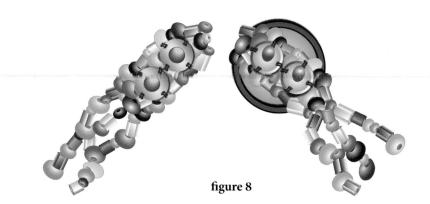

figure 8

Carol Perrenoud is a bead artist, teacher, and entrepreneur. Her work has been exhibited nationally and featured in many books. She has penned articles for *Bead&Button* and *Beadwork* magazines and has authored four instructional videos: *Beadweaving Peyote Stitch, Bead Crochet, Bead Embroidery, and Beadweaving Herringbone Stitch.* In 2002, she received Bead&Button's Excellence in Bead Artistry award with Virginia Blakelock. Many of her pieces reference animals she studied while a zoology student in college, but her interest in beads and fibers is lifelong. Carol spends days working in her mail-order business, Beadcats, and her evenings recovering and gardening— sometimes by headlamp. She is active in the Portland Bead Society. Visit her website, beadcats.com.

Virginia Blakelock grew up as a painter, but finds that beads have completely seduced her. She likes their small scale, and the two- and three-dimensional complexity which they make possible. She likes the permanence of color, and that she can hold them in her hands and play with them. Her work is a dialogue, fight, and/or collaboration between herself and the piece. Works evolve slowly over time, sometimes taking years to complete because the beading process itself is so slow. She looks at nature and at the historical and indigenous art and craft of the world for inspiration. She's interested in creating complex, beautiful objects that will transcend her, our culture, and this time.

Photo: Gary Lee Betts

An Oregon Bouquet

Since we both use nature as our muse, a botanical theme leapt to mind. Oregonians are very outdoorsy and we have a love/hate relationship with our native and non-native undergrowth. The blackberry cheers us in the summer and connects us to our roots as we stand by the vine and pick and eat only the very ripe ones. At the same time, blackberries have horrible thorns and will take over pastures, farm vehicles, and even grow over entire houses! So, after we pick blackberries in season to freeze for cobbler in the winter, we curse and bandage our fingers as we hack and chop our way to reclaim the pastures. Imagine the juxtaposition of killing them by day and then designing and making this beaded rendition for you to enjoy at night. And ferns—you know ferns need to grow where it rains all the time! We would have included a slug or two, but we thought the piece was getting crowded.

stitch
tubular brick, herringbone, St. Petersburg chain
level
advanced

supplies
Blackberries
- 8º seed beads
  5 g A: dark purple opaque iridescent
  2.5 g B: cranberry transparent luster
- Size 10 beading needles
- Nymo E or F thread, black

Blackberry Calyx
- 8º seed beads
  15 C: olive opaque matte iridescent
  15 D: tan matte iridescent
- 11º seed beads
  45 C: olive opaque matte iridescent
  45 D: tan matte iridescent
- 15º seed beads
  45 C: olive opaque matte iridescent
  45 D: tan matte iridescent
- Size 12 beading needles
- Nymo B or KO B thread, gold or natural

Blackberry Flower
- 9 mm Czech pressed glass flowers with five petals and center hole
  2 opal pink
  2 white
- 10 11º seed beads E: green-gold opaque matte metallic iridescent
- 15º seed beads
  8 P: any color
  8 N: light amber transparent iridescent
- Nymo B thread, gold
- Size 13 beading needles
- Brown permanent marker

Fern Fronds
- 11º seed beads
  41 L: olive transparent with heavy bronze luster
  33 H: olive transparent luster
  33 J: light yellow-green transparent lined with gold
- 15º seed beads
  17 J: light yellow-green transparent lined with gold
  2 g F: in aqua transparent lined with gold
  115 G: green transparent with olive-gold luster
  41 M: clear lined with metallic tan, iridescent
  41 K: green transparent lined with black, iridescent
- Nymo B or KO B thread, olive and gold
- Size 13 beading needles

Assembly
- **100** 11º seed beads E: green-gold matte metallic iridescent
- **32** 15º seed beads E: green-gold matte metallic iridescent
- Nymo D or KO B thread, gold and black
- Size 13 beading needles
- **2** gold tie tacks with holes in the bases
- Ultrasuede, gold
- 1 ft. 28-gauge gold-filled wire

Blackberries
1. Thread a needle onto 2 ft. of thread. Make an eight-bead ladder with Color A, leaving an 8-in. tail. Join the ends to form a ring.
2. Work three rounds of brick stitch using eight As in each round (**figure 1**).
3. Decrease, working one round with six As (**figure 1**).
4. Decrease again, working one round with four As (**figure 1**).
5. Close the top with one A. Weave the thread into the body of the blackberry, and trim.
6. Thread a needle onto the 8-in. tail, and bead a row of brick stitch using the color in the first row. Pull the bottom tight while stitching. It's OK to decrease by one bead to make the piece tighter. Weave in the tail and trim (**figure 2**).
7. Make a total of three blackberries with Color A.
8. Make one blackberry with Color B.
9. Make one blackberry beginning with a B in Steps 1–2 and ending with an A in Steps 3–4.
10. Make a smaller blackberry beginning with six 8ºs. Start by alternating colors A and B in the round. Stitch another round of six beads using A, A, B, A, A, B. Using color A, work one round of five beads, one round of three beads, and close the top with one A.

Blackberry calyx
11. Thread a needle onto 2 ft. of thread. Tie a figure-8 knot 6 in. from the end. Pointing away from the center of the blackberry, put the needle under a blackberry thread, and pull until the knot snags. Tie a half-hitch knot around the blackberry thread to secure, and trim the tail.

> Use color C on the unripe blackberries (made with some or all Bs) and color D on the ripe blackberries (made with all As).

12. Work a round of brick stitch using 10 C 15ºs on the bottom of the blackberry. Since the average blackberry has seven to eight beads, add two C 15ºs in a couple of the stitches to fill in the space. Draw the circle up snug. Join the end of the row to its beginning by going down through the first C 15º and then back through the last C 15º (**figure 3**).
13. Work one round of herringbone stitch with eight C 11ºs (**figure 4**).

14. Sew up through the first C 11º. Pick up a C 8º, a C 11º, and a C 15º. Sew back through the 11º and 8º and down through the second half of the herringbone stitch. Continue all the way around (**figure 5**).

Making the blackberry attachment point

15. Coming out of a 15º from Step 12, pick up three C 11ºs. Sew through the C 15º on the opposite side of the calyx base. Go up through another 15º, 90 degrees from the first three 11ºs. Pick up one C 11º. Sew through the middle C 11º of the original three. Pick up a C 11º. Sew through the C 15º. Secure the thread, and trim (**figure 6**).

Blackberry flower

16. Start a new thread. Pick up three E 11ºs and the pink opal flower. Pick up four N 15ºs and sew down through the hole in the flower and the closest E 11º. Pull the ring down tight to make a loop (**figure 7**).

17. Go around the E 11º closest to the flower and sew up through the flower's hole. Put the needle under the thread loop between the second and third E 15ºs. Sew down through the flower's hole and the E 11º just below. Pull the thread snug to flatten the ring of E 15ºs (**figure 8**).

18. Going around the top 11º stem bead, sew up through the flower's hole. Make sure the thread comes up inside the ring of E 15ºs (**figure 9**).

Stamens

19. Cut 1 ft. of gold thread. Coil 3–4 wraps of thread around your little finger with both tails pointing in the same direction. Carefully slide the thread coils off your finger, and sew through them (**figure 9**).

20. Hold the thread coils with the fingers of one hand and sew down through the 15º ring, the flower's hole, and all the stem beads. Pull gently but firmly to anchor the coil of thread. It will "click" when in place. Bring the thread back into the branch to continue to assemble the bouquet (**figure 9**).

21. Cut the thread coils about ³⁄₁₆ in. above the surface of the flower, and color the tips with a brown permanent marker.

22. The next two flowers you will pick up are the white opal ones, using color P 15ºs for the centers. The final flower is pink opal. Follow steps 16–21 to make these remaining flowers.

figure 1   figure 2   figure 3

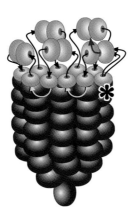

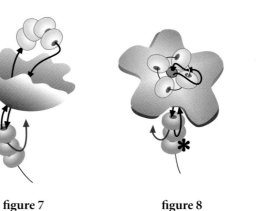

figure 4   figure 5   figure 6

figure 7   figure 8   figure 9

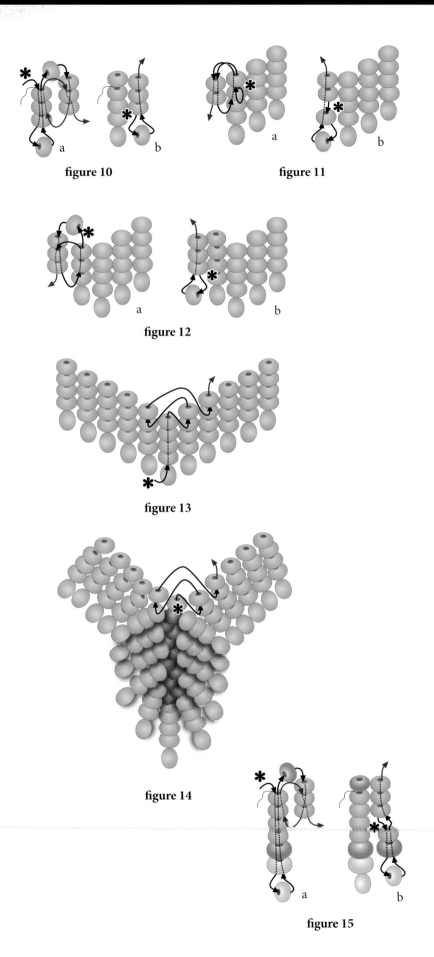

figure 10

figure 11

figure 12

figure 13

figure 14

Fern frond one (right side)

23. Thread a needle onto 6 ft. of olive thread. Pick up four F 15°s. Skip one bead, and sew back through three beads. Center this fringe on the thread. **Note:** This is a center stitch only and is not included in the counts for the right and left sides (**figure 10a**).

24. Pick up four F 15°s. Sew up through the top two F 15°s of the previous stitch. Go down through the last two beads of the current stitch (**figure 10a**).

25. Pick up one F 15°. Sew back up through three F 15°s of the current stitch (**figure 10b**).

26. Repeat Steps 24–25 for a total of 28 stitches.

Fern frond one (left side)

27. Thread a needle onto the tail thread. Sew up through the top bead of the center stitch. Pick up two F 15°s. Sew up through the top two F 15°s in the center stitch and down through the two beads just added (**figure 11a**).

28. Pick up two F 15°s, skip one F 15° and go back through the first F 15° just added and the upper two beads of the current stitch (**figure 11b**).

29. Pick up four F 15°s. Sew up through the last two beads of the stitch just completed and down through the last two F 15°s just added (**figure 12a**).

30. Pick up one F 15°. Sew up through the three beads of the current stitch (**figure 12b**).

31. Repeat Steps 29–30 26 more times for a total of 28 stitches.

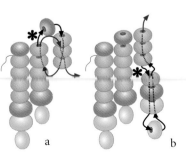

figure 15

figure 16

Zip the frond

32. Thread a needle onto 1 ft. of thread, and tie an overhand knot at one end.

33. Insert the needle into the center frond stitch. Snag the knot in one of the frond F 15°s (**figure 13**).

34. Sew all the way through the remaining beads of this stitch. Sew up through the last bead of the stitch on the immediate right of the frond center stitch. Sew up through the last F 15° of the stitch on the immediate left of the frond center stitch. Pull the thread tight (**figure 13**).

35. Continue sewing through the final F 15° of each stitch alternating sides, pulling the stitches tight every two to three beads until reaching the end. Secure and trim all but one tail. The beads from each side should lock into place down the center of the frond, just like a zipper (**figure 14**).

All fern fronds are constructed the same, but the amounts and colors of beads and the number of stitches are different.

Fern frond two (right side)

36. Thread a needle onto 6 ft. of gold thread. Pick up four F 15°s, one H 11°, one J 11°, and one J 15°. Skip the last J 15°, and sew back through the other beads. Center on the thread (**figure 15a**).

37. Pick up one G 15° and three F 15°s. Follow Step 24 (**figure 15a**).

38. Pick up one F 15°, one H 11°, and one J 15°. Skip the J 15°, and sew back through the other five beads (**figure 15b**).

39. Pick up one G 15° and three F 15°s. Follow Step 22 (**figure 16a**).

40. Pick up one F 15°, one H 11°, one J 11°, and one J 15°. Skip the J 15° and sew through the six other beads of the current stitch (**figure 16b**).

41. Follow Steps 37–40 until there are 16 stitches in total. You will be alternating between the stringing sequences in steps 38 and 40 (Step 40 has one more 11°).

Fern frond two (left side)

42. Follow Step 27.

43. Pick up two F 15°s, one H 11°, and one F 15°, and complete the stitch as in step 28.

44. Follow Steps 37–40 for 15 more stitches, once again alternating between the two stringing sequences.

45. Follow Steps 32–35 to zip the frond.

Fern frond three (right side)

46. Thread a needle onto 6 ft. of thread, and pick up one K 15°, two G 15°s, one L 11°, one F 15° and one M 15°. Skip the M 15°, and sew back through all the other beads. Center on the thread (**figure 17a**).

47. Pick up one G 15°, one K 15°, and two G 15°s. Follow figure 17a to complete the first half of this stitch.

48. Pick up one L 11°, one F 15°, and one M 15°. Follow figure 17b to complete the stitch. Work 19 more stitches using this sequence (**figures 17a and 17b**).

Fern frond three (left side)

49. Follow **figure 18a** using two G 15°s .

50. Pick up one G 15°, one L 11°, one F 15°, and one M 15°. Follow **figure 18b** to complete the stitch. Note: This stringing sequence differs from the right side.

51. Pick up one K 15° and three G 15°s and follow **figure 19** until there are 20 stitches in total to complete this side of the frond.

52. Follow Steps 32–35 to zip the frond.

Assembling the bouquet

53. Thread a needle onto 3 ft. of gold thread and pick up one E 11° as a stop bead, leaving a 6-in. tail. Pick up 51 more E 11°s. Choose a dark purple blackberry, and sew through its center "attachment" bead. Pick up another E 11°, skip the 51st bead, and sew back through the next four E 11°s on the branch. Keep the tension tight (**figure 20**).

54. Make a thorn by picking up three E 15°s. Skip the last E 15°, and sew back through the next one. Pick up another E 15° and re-enter the branch. Sew through the same E 11° branch bead or skip a E 11°, and sew through the next one (**figure 20**).

55. Sew through two more beads on the branch, and pick up one opal-pink flower, Go up through the stem beads and flower. Go under the thread loop between the 15°s and back down the stem (**figure 8**).

56. Skip one branch bead, go through the next bead, and make a thorn as in Step 54.

57. Sew through two more branch beads, and attach a dark purple berry with a 6-bead stem. To make the stem, pick up seven E 11°s. Sew through the attachment bead on the base of the berry. Pick up one more E 11°, and re-enter the stem, skipping the last bead. Keep the tension tight (**figure 21**).

58. Sew through three E 11°s (branch beads) and make a thorn. Re-enter the branch through the very next E 11°.

Completing the pin

59. Sew through three E 11°s, and add an opal flower with a three-bead stem (Step 55).

60. Sew through three more E 11°s, and pick up one dark purple blackberry with a six-bead stem and add a thorn.

61. Sew through three more E 11°s, and pick up one thorn.

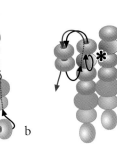
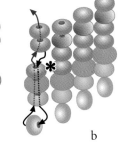

figure 17

figure 18

figure 19

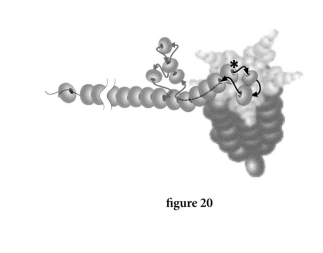

figure 20

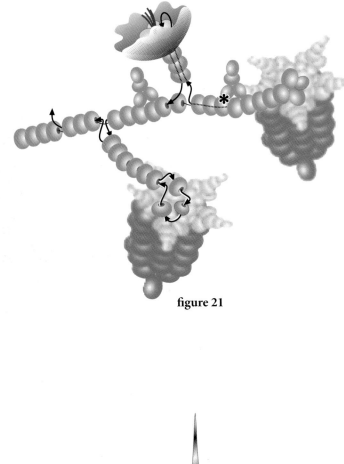

figure 21

figure 22

62. Sew through three E 11º beads, and add the small blackberry with a five-bead stem.

63. Sew through five E 11º branch beads, and add a thorn.

64. Sew through three E 11º branch beads, and add the dark purple and cranberry berry, with a six-bead stem.

65. Sew through two E 11º branch beads, and add a thorn.

66. Sew through two E 11º branch beads, and pick up one opal white flower on a two-bead stem (Step 55).

67. Sew through two E 11º branch beads, and add the cranberry blackberry with a six-bead stem.

68. Sew through three E 11º branch beads, and pick up one opal-pink flower on a two-bead stem (Step 55).

69. Sew through the remainder of the branch. Tie the ends of the thread together, and use later to attach the tie tack and fronds.

Finishing

70. Cut two circles of Ultrasuede the size of the tie tack base. Slip one circle over the pin, and hold the other circle against the flat side. Whip stitch the pieces together around the edges, using the gold thread. Cover only one tie tack in this way **(figure 22)**.

71. Insert 28-gauge wire into the branch beads and into the center lines of the fern fronds. Use a slightly longer piece than necessary and trim the ends with small wire cutters.

72. Using the extra branch thread, sew the fern fronds and the end of the branch stem to the first tie tack (fronds 1 and 2 first pointing in different directions and then frond 3 and the branch). Secure, and trim this thread.

73. Thread a needle onto a comfortable length of black Nymo D thread, and sew the last berry to the second tie tack. Color any visible edges of the tie tack with black marker. It's advisable to slightly flatten the blackberry as you sew it down, to hide the tie tack.

Stephanie Eddy has been creating beads and jewelry designs for over 35 years. She works in media including glass fusing and blowing, stained glass, pottery, wirework, welding, fibers, watercolor, floral design, enameling, and sculpture. Stephanie created and patented the Lazee Daizee Viking Knit all-in-one tool. Her free-form wire design, *One Man's Pond Scum*, won the 2009 Popular Vote in an Internet-wide wire-sculpture competition. Stephanie teaches across the U. S. and internationally at the Kobe Japan Art Show. Her beadwork has been displayed at the Tokyo Art Metropolitan Museum's Zen Exhibition, publications, and she has appeared in televised episodes of *Beads, Baubles & Jewels*. See Stephanie's work at stephanieeddy.com.

Tri-Flora Exotica Necklace

Idaho, the Gem State, produces 72 types of precious and semiprecious stones. The acreage surrounding my home and studio is abundant with design possibilities and inspiration, with flowing waterways, floral landscapes, and multicolored forest canopies that offer sanctuary to a variety of wildlife. My favorite time is late summer when dragonflies and mayflies hatch into spiral patterns of grace and color across the ponds. The best thing about Idaho is that it's big, uncrowded, and unpretentious. I live in Garden City, a suburb of Boise, the City of Trees. I view my home as a city of colors and Idaho as my state of mind: A place where I gain unlimited inspiration and the serenity to create and design unhampered.

stitches
herringbone, peyote, daisy chain
level
intermediate

supplies
- 11º seed beads
    - **14 g** A: light green
    - **4.5 g** B: dark pink
    - **4.5 g** C: light pink
    - **8.5 g** D: white
    - **14 g** E: dark green
    - **14 g** F: pearl
    - **8.5 g** G: maroon
- Size 12 beading needles
- Nymo B or C-Lon thread
- **3** 6 mm round clear acrylic or glass beads
- **6** 3 mm round pink fire-polished beads

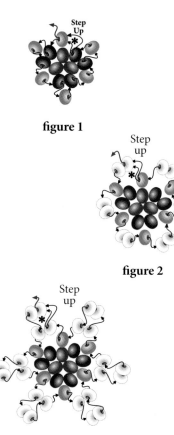

figure 1

figure 2

figure 3

Flower one (make three)

1. Thread a needle onto 1 yd. of thread. Pick up three Es. Go back through the Es to form a circle.

2. Pick up two Gs between each E from the previous row. Step up to begin the next row. Stitch one row of even-count peyote stitch by adding one B between each G from the previous row. Step up at the end of the row (**figure 1**).

3. Begin two-drop peyote. Pick up two Fs between each B in the previous row. Step up to begin the next row (**figure 2**).

4. Repeat Step 3. Pick up two Fs, go down through one F and B, and up through one F in the previous row. Repeat the pattern all the way around. Step up as before (**figure 3**).

5. Pick up two Fs and work one herringbone stitch. Pick up one A between herringbone stitches on that row. Go up through the F in the previous row, Repeat the pattern all the way around (**figure 4**).

6. Pick up two Fs, and do one herringbone stitch. Go down the next two Fs from the previous row, though the A and up through the following two Fs (**figure 5**). Repeat all the way around.

7. Pick up two Fs, and work one regular herringbone stitch. Continue down two Fs. Pick up two As between the herringbone stitches in that row. Go up through the next two Fs of the previous row. Repeat all the way around (**figure 6**).

8. Pick up two Fs, and work a herringbone stitch. Continue down three Fs. Continue up through the first A in the previous row. Pick up two As. Go down the next A from the previous row and up through the following three Fs. Repeat around (**figure 7**).

9. Pick up one B, one G, and one B. Make a picot on top of the herringbone row of Fs. Go down through four Fs and up through the next two As from the previous row. Pick up three As and go down through two As and up through the following four Fs. Repeat around (**figure 8**).

10. Sew toward the center, and tie the working thread with the tail. Secure the thread (**figure 8**).

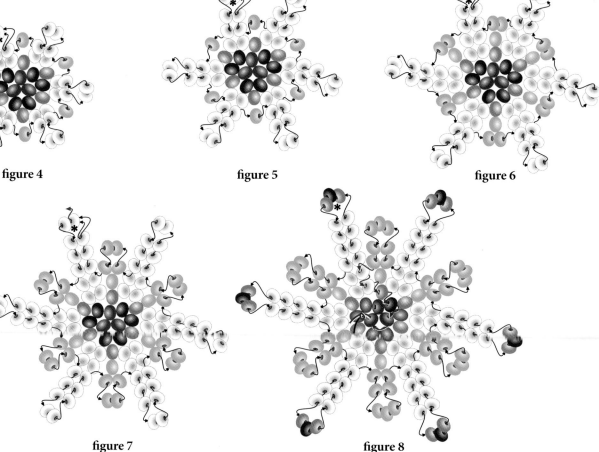

figure 4

figure 5

figure 6

figure 7

figure 8

Flower two (make two)

11. Repeat Steps 1–4.

12. Follow Steps 5–8, using G in place of A.

13. Pick up one E, one A, and one E between each two Fs. Continue down four Fs and up through the next two Gs from the previous row. Pick up one G, one B, one C, one B, and one G. Go down two Gs and up through the following four Fs. Repeat around (**figure 9**).

14. Sew back through each C tip bead (**figure 9**). Place a 6 mm round bead into the center before closing the center. This will help hold the shape (**figure 10**). Reinforce the circle. End the thread as in Step 10.

Flower three (make six)

15. Repeat Steps 1–4, using D in place of F.

16. Follow Steps 5–8, substituting E in place of A.

17. Pick up one G, one C, and one G between the two Ds of the previous row to make a picot. Continue down four Ds and up through the next two Es from the previous row. Add three Es, and go down two Es and up through the following four Ds. Repeat around (**figure 11**).

18. Sew back through each C tip bead (**figure 11**), and close the center. Reinforce the circle. Pick up one 3 mm round crystal across the top. End the thread as in Step 10 (**figure 12**).

Make the chain

19. Pick up six Es. Go back through the beads to make a circle. Tie the tail and working thread together (**figure 13**).

20. Pick up one A. Bring the thread directly across the circle. Place the A in the middle of the circle and press it into place. There should be three 11ºs on each side of the lead thread. Sew through one 11º to the left of the thread (**figure 13**).

21. Pick up four Es, and go into the right side of the next bead to form a circle. Pick up one A and place it in the middle of the circle. Bring the thread across the circle through one E (**figure 14**).

22. Repeat Step 21 until the chain is approximately 3-in. long.

Assemble the flowers

23. Attach the flowers in the following sequence: 3, 1, 3, 2, 3, 1, 3, 2, 3, 1, 3

24. Attach the flowers to the chain with daisy chain stitch. Pick up three Es and the tip of a flower, creating a circle as in Step 21. Pick up one A in the middle (**figure 15**).

25. Once the flowers are attached, continue making the chain to the desired length. Work the chain from both sides to center the flowers. Leave a 12–18 in. tail.

Make the clasp

26. Attach the remaining flower number two to one end to act as a button. Stitch a loop on the other end large enough to accommodate the flower. Secure the threads.

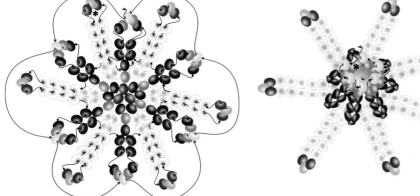

figure 9

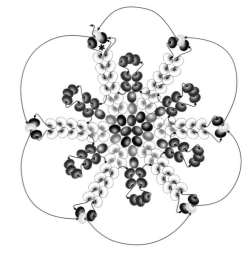

figure 10

figure 11

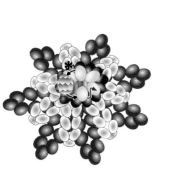

figure 12

figure 13

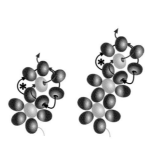

figure 14

figure 15

Huib Petersen was first drawn to needlecrafts as a child growing up in Holland. He picked up knitting, tatting, macramé, embroidery, and more with ease. After moving to San Francisco in 1995, he was inspired by 19th century Russian beadwork and discovered the beauty and challenges of designing with beads. Different bead sizes and a variety of traditional stitches help him create sculpted bugs, butterflies, birds, flowers, and sea creatures in their environment. The result is a unique kind of wearable art that offers the intricacy of embroidery and lace, the depth of a theater set, and the durability and brilliance of glass. See more of Huib's work at petersenarts.com.

California Poppy

stitch
two-drop peyote, flat and tubular peyote, tubular herringbone
level
advanced

supplies
- 15º seed beads
  - **10 g** A: orange
  - **10 g** B: matte green seed beads
- 11º seed beads
  - **30 g** C: matte green
- One G thread
- Size 12 or 13 beading needles

I find my inspiration in the irrepressible natural world that persists in this dense city. I like how beadwork can capture the light in the same way as a water lily floating in a pond or a butterfly flittering past—especially when the beadwork is worn, rather than left to rest in a display case. In this piece, I honor the California poppies that bloom every spring in the cracks in the sidewalk along our street, shocking passersby to attention with their brilliant orange.

Flower petals (make four)

1. Thread a needle onto 2½ yds. of thread. Put a stop bead at the middle. Wrap half the thread around a bobbin, and set aside for the bottom half of the petal.

The chart for the petal is shown in two colors for visual purposes only (figure 1).

2. To start Rows 1 and 2 pick up 26 As. Work in two-drop odd and even-count peyote (**figure 1**). Once the first petal half is complete (Rows 1–29), thread a needle onto the reserved thread, and finish the other half of the petal (Rows A–X) (**figure 2**).

The petal edges of the two-drop peyote often split, and at times no beads are added. Watch for turnarounds, and remember to position the thread in order to add beads in the next row.

3. Leave the longer thread tail in place. Secure and cut the shorter thread.

Edging the petals

4. Use the thread tail to edge the tops of each petal with As as shown on the graph (**figure 3**).

Flower bud (make one)

5. The bud is a taller version of the flower petals created in Steps 1 and 2. Thread a needle onto 4 yds. of thread, leaving a 1-yd. tail. Set aside for the bottom of the bud. Pick up 26 As. Starting at Row 1, repeat Rows 1–4 six times for a total of 28 rows of two-drop peyote. This is what makes the bud broader than the flower petals (**figure 4**).

6. Follow the graph (**figure 4**) to complete the bud. Rows 1–57 make the top of the bud. Rows A–X (**figure 1**) make the bottom of the bud. Remember, the petal edges split and at times no beads are added.

7. Once the bud is complete, edge the top of the bud following figure 3.

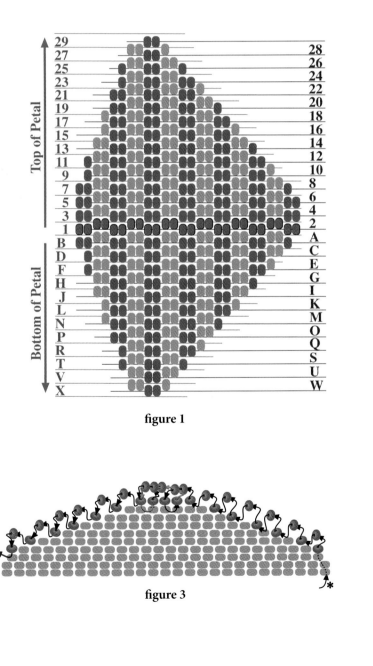

figure 1

figure 3

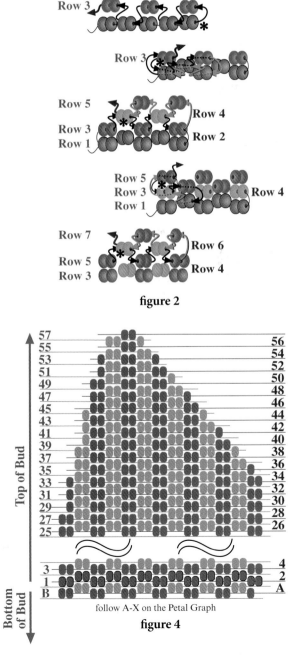

figure 2

follow A-X on the Petal Graph

figure 4

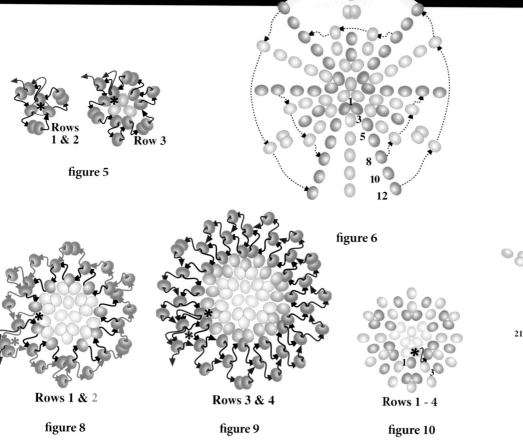

figure 5

Rows 1 & 2   Row 3

figure 6

figure 7

Rows 1 & 2
figure 8

Rows 3 & 4
figure 9

Rows 1 - 4
figure 10

Rows 11 - 21
figure 11

On the top of the bud, use two beads to edge the right side and one bead to edge the left side.

Calyx (make six)
8. Thread a needle onto 2 yds. of thread leaving a 1-yd. tail for later use.
Row 1: Pick up three Bs, and go through the first 15º strung to make a circle (**figure 5**).
Row 2: Increase by adding two Bs between each 15º in the circle (add 6 beads). Step up to start the next row (**figure 5**).
Row 3: Split the increases with one bead, and pick up two beads between the increases for a total of nine beads (**figure 5**).
Rows 4–7: Work in regular peyote with 9 beads in each row. Step up after each row. Pull Rows 5 and 6 tight for the calyx to take its 3-D shape (**figure 6**).
Row 8: Decrease by three beads (see figure 6 for placement of decreases)
Row 9: Pick up two beads on top of decrease, one bead between (**figure 6**).
Rows 10 and 11: Work in regular peyote (**figure 6**). (There are six beads in each row.)

In Row 10, treat the two Bs together from Row 9 as one. Do not split these.

Row 12: Decrease by four beads. Go through all four beads again.
9. Begin tubular herringbone using Cs for 1 in. Leave the remaining thread hanging and put it to the side. You may want to add more herringbone rope later (**figure 7**).

Calyx collar (make six)
10. Thread a needle onto the remaining thread from Step 8, and begin tubular peyote from Row 4 of the calyx, using Bs.
Row 1: three increases (12 beads) (**figure 8**).
Row 2: three increases (15 beads) (✻ **figure 8**).
Row 3: regular peyote row (15 beads).
Row 4: three increases (18 beads) (✻ **figure 9**). Pass through several beads, secure the thread, and cut.

Seed pods (make four varying in size)
11. Thread a needle onto 2½ yds. of thread, leaving an 8-in. tail. Pick up a calyx, and secure the new thread to it. Exit at Row 2 of the calyx (above the collar) to begin the pod. (Use longer thread for larger seed pods and shorter thread for smaller ones.)

12. Start tubular peyote stitch from Row 2 with Bs, watching carefully for the decreases as the pod progresses (Rows 1–4 **figure 10**). Rows 5–10 are regular peyote.
13. Follow figure 11 for Rows 11–21.

Create the seed pod like the calyx. Follow the graph for rows and thread paths. To change size, increase or decrease peyote rows starting at Row 4. For a smaller pod, stitch to row 6 or 7, then skip to Rows 11–21 for the decrease. For a medium pod, stitch to Row 8 or 9, then skip to Rows 11–21 for the decrease. For a large pod, stitch to row 10 or 11, then skip to rows 11–21 for the decrease. Use additional rows of regular peyote at Rows 13, 17 and 20 to maintain the shape.

Joining the flower petals and bud to each calyx
14. The flower petals and bud are joined to each calyx in the same way. Zip the bud to the calyx starting in the middle of Row 3 and working out toward Row 4. Zip each petal to another calyx at Row 4. Reinforce the connections. Once the flowers are attached, weave in the thread, tie half-hitch knots to secure, and cut.

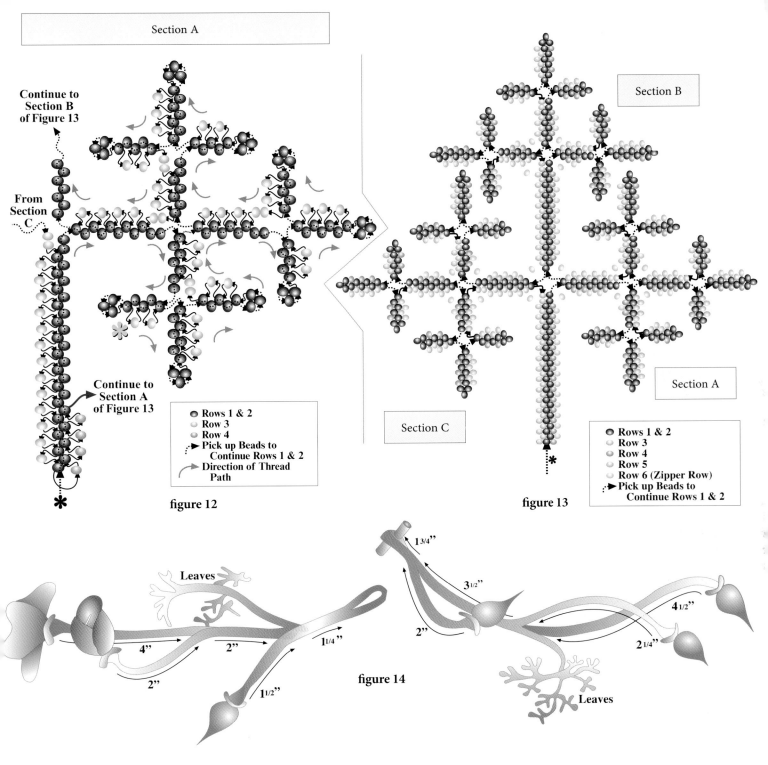

Section A

Continue to
Section B
of Figure 13

From
Section
C

Continue to
Section A
of Figure 13

● Rows 1 & 2
○ Row 3
● Row 4
·▸ Pick up Beads to
    Continue Rows 1 & 2
➔ Direction of Thread
    Path

figure 12

Section B

Section C

Section A

● Rows 1 & 2
○ Row 3
○ Row 4
○ Row 5
○ Row 6 (Zipper Row)
·▸ Pick up Beads to
    Continue Rows 1 & 2

figure 13

Leaves

1 3/4"

3 1/2"

4 1/2"

4"

2"

1 1/4"

2"

2"

2 1/4"

1 1/2"

figure 14

Leaves

Leaves (make two)

15. Thread a needle onto 4 yds. of thread, leaving an 8-in. tail.

16. Pick up 55 Bs, and work in flat even-count peyote stitch following the diagram. Start peyote stitch by adding Row 3 (**figure 12** ✳).

The graph for the leaves are shown in multiple colors for visual purposes only (figures 12 and 13).

17. Once Rows 1–5 are completed, work Row 6 of flat peyote stitch with Bs to the right side of each stem (**figure 13**).

18. Zip Row 6 beads to Row 5. The outer edges of the leaves remain flat and do not get zipped.

Putting the piece together

19. With Cs, work in tubular herringbone to create the connecting stems used throughout the piece. See the diagram

(**figure 14**) for the dimensions. Adjust the length of the herringbone rope as needed.

20. Put together the first half of the piece, then stitch a loop at the top to create a toggle ring for the closure.

21. After constructing the second half of the piece, make a tubular herringbone bar 20 rows long to use as the toggle. Finish with a picot edge on each side of the toggle bar.

Alethia Donathan has designed her own line of jewelry since 1991. Her creations are unique and recognized throughout the bead and jewelry community. For more information, visit her website, dacsbeads.com

Lei Haku Necklace

Falling in love with beads and traveling extensively to buy inventory for my store revealed the world of handmade glass beads. Soon I was hooked and behind the torch making my own. As a full-time lampworker, I find the craft to be both work and play; it's about the process and final product, and is a passion and an obsession. Many of my beads are inspired by the textures, natural beauty, and mystique of the islands, while others, such as the Na Ki'I Pohaku Series, preserve Hawaii's history. By combining my own blends of frits, enamels, and metal foils, I can capture the look of sand or the image of a hot lava flow. I often incorporate these unique beads into jewelry that is braided using an ancient Japanese weaving technique known as Kumihimo.

stitch
macramé
level
all levels

supplies
- Art glass floral focal set (dacsbeads.com)
   3 15 mm art glass accent flowers with center holes
   4 art glass accent flowers
   2 leaves
- **2** 8 mm large-holed beads
- **8** 5 mm SWAROVSKI ELEMENTS crystal bicones in assorted colors
- **20–30** assorted pressed glass flowers and leaves with top-drilled large holes
- **10–50** g of various sizes and colors of seed beads
- Clasp
- 4 in. 6 mm chain
- **2** 4 mm ID end caps with loop
- **4** 4 mm open jump rings
- 15 yds. Mastex Thread
- Power Pro, 10-lb. test
- Size 12 sharps needles
- Macramé board
- Scrap piece of poster board
- E-6000 adhesive
- G-S Hypo Cement
- T-pin

Measuring and setting up the materials

1. Cut five 1-yd. strands of Mastex for the core cords. Cut one 10-yd. strand for the knotting cord.

2. Coat the ends of the cord with G-S Hypo cement. Cut the ends on a point when dry. Line up one end of all the core cords and make an overhand knot about three in. from the end. Pin it onto a macramé board.

3. Center the knotting cord under the core bundle below the knot, and tie an overhand knot around the core cords. To prevent the knotting thread from tangling, wrap each end onto a 3-in. scrap of poster board (**figure 1**).

Making the necklace

4. Work 2 in. of square macramé knots.

> Don't weave the macramé stitches too tight, as it will be difficult to embellish.

5. Slide one 8 mm bead over all the core cords, twisting them to make it easier to slide the bead on. Push the bead close to the last knot but not so tight that the piece will bunch up. Make an overhand knot with all the cords.

6. Tie ½ in. of half knots, creating a twisted spiral.

7. String an accent flower bead, a 5 mm crystal, and an 11º seed bead onto one of the core cords. Take this cord back through the crystal and flower bead to form a picot (**figure 2**).

8. Tie another ½ in. of half knots.

9. String on another accent flower bead, and tie another ½ in. of half knots.

10. String the first large flower bead over all the core cords, as in Step 5.

11. Tie 1 in. of half knots.

12. Put on one art glass leaf. Put the core strand through the hole.

13. Tie 1 in. of half knots.

14. Pick up the center flower bead and repeat Step 10.

15. Reverse Steps 5–13 and end by tying 2 in. of square/flat knots.

16. To end the macramé, tie an overhand knot with all of the cords. Leave the cords in place.

Embellishing the macramé

17. Divide the remaining pressed glass flowers and leaves into two groups. Thread a needle onto 2 yds. of Power Pro, and tie a large overhand knot as close to the end as possible.

18. Sew through the macramé just below the first 8 mm bead and attach a flower or leaf. Continue until you reach the opposite end. Secure the thread in the macramé, and end it (**figure 3**).

19. Thread a needle onto 2 yds. of Power Pro. Tie a large overhand knot as close to the end of the thread as possible. Pick up 6 or more 8's in any colors. Starting below the first accent bead, sew through the macramé. Make loops of assorted seed beads all the way to the opposite end of the piece. Use your creativity, and embellish as desired. Secure the thread in the macramé, and end it.

20. Dip the ends of the macramé into E-6000, and insert the knot into the end cap. Let it set for 24 hours.

21. Add the jump rings to the end cap. Attach the chain extension and clasp.

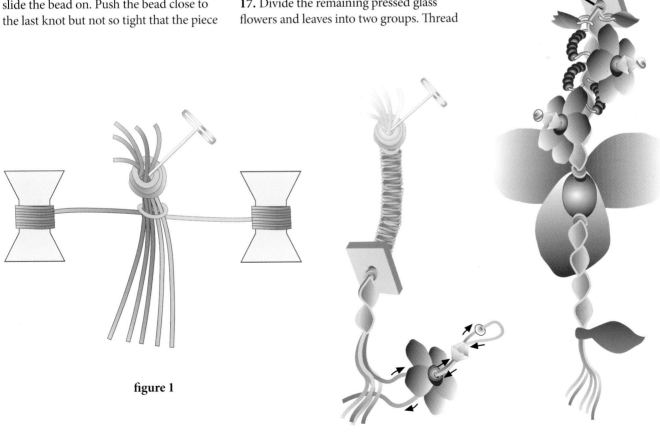

figure 1

figure 2

figure 3

MARYLAND Paulette Baron

VIRGINIA Amy Katz

PENNSYLVANIA Sherry Serafini

Art has always been my love. From paintings to printmaking to vivid drawings, everything about art has defined me and how I see the world. As a result, I pursued my Fine Arts degree at Carnegie Mellon University in drawing and illustration and began a career as an illustrator.

As time went on, art became even a greater part of my persona. While I thought I had explored just about every aspect, the biggest surprise came as a birthday gift. My friend and co-author Amy Katz gave me a pair of beaded earrings that she had made. As soon as I pulled those earrings out of the box, I knew I found the medium I had been seeking as an artist, and I wanted to explore it from every angle.

In my beadwork quest, I not only learned to be creative, but sculptural. In traditional sculpture the idea of finishing the back of the piece never really registered with me. With beads the pieces became unified and the sculptor in me was born. It led me to experiment with different sizes and shapes of beads and it turned my world from flat to dimensional. I now call myself a sculptural bead artist.

Perhaps the most defining moment of my career was being asked to illustrate *Beading Across America*. Throughout the process, not only was I able to express myself sculpturally, but I was given the palette of this beautiful book to create and draw.

Years ago I started to bead as a hobby, and eventually, it became my passion. As my love for beads grew, I began to explore the true depths of beadwork by learning from others who were equally as passionate. After absorbing techniques from various resources and developing my own, I came into my style.

Once I realized that I myself was a bead artist, I wanted to do more than create beautiful pieces. It was my goal to share the collective work. To me the beauty of bead art is that it is a global community. Through teaching it has been my greatest fortune to share my ideas with people across the nation and from around the world. Each time I teach, I also take a little piece of knowledge with me from those who came to learn. This is a true gift and one that beadwork community continually gives.

The journey has been particularly special for me since I am a student, a teacher, and an artist, but it doesn't end here. To truly emerge myself in the work, the process of growing and learning must perpetually continue. As it does, self-satisfaction arises which brings me the joy of accomplishment.

While I cannot describe this feeling, I can present it. Co-authoring *Beading Across America* has been my way to continue this journey, not only by presenting my own work but the work of many who have had an impact on my art.

Unusual objects and shapes become part of a new story as I stitch beads and gemstones, one at a time, to a felt-like base. Most pieces are born spontaneously as the beads and my imagination dictate the design. I seldom work from sketches. I have a degree in graphic design and studied fine art, which I feel influences the beadwork I create.

To me, this meditative form of art is a rich counterpoint to a society full of instant gratification.

My journey into the bead world started with tragedy rather than joy. Years ago, my mother was in a serious car accident. Our family spent countless weeks sitting in the hospital monitoring her progress. I needed to keep busy during this waiting time. So I picked up some beads and cloth and began stitching. I had no intention of creating art. I was trying to keep my mind occupied at a time when it was difficult to think.

My mother survived the accident, and while it wasn't intentional, I found myself on a new path as well. Through my exploration, I found a new sense of creativity that changed the meaning of art as I knew it forever. My reason for co-authoring *Beading Across America* is to give readers the sense of how to discover your own inner artist. All 30 artists found their own path and while the paths are different, the love of beadwork is a common thread for all.

Thank You

Thank you to the many skilled seed bead artists and enthusiasts who helped us test the projects for this book. Your help was an extraordinary contribution.

Thanks to the gang at Bead Obsessions in Alexandria, Va.: Owner Patricia Woodhouse, Susan Wenzel, Sherry Ellis, Danielle Castelo, Rebecca Hoop, Roxanne Rash, Lorri Tunney, Marsha Ray, Doreen Jagodnik, Linda Armstrong, Cathy Ryan, and Valerie Friend.

Special thanks to all who sat at home and tested the projects individually: Beth Eltinge, Lynda Horsman, Patti Feit, Sandy Houk, Katie Nelson, Carrie Johnson, Lisa Uribe, Sheeler Kowalewski, Denise Rivers, Margaret Shannon Test, Pamela E. Troutman, Marie Campbell, Laura Beaty, and Lisa Norris.

Dedications

Paulette Baron:
To my Mother, for your coffee table in heaven. To Michael, Hannah, and Zach, for putting up with me during all of the hours I spend in my Bead Cave and allowing me to follow my creative dream.

Amy Katz:
To Rick, Andrew, and Melissa—you are my inspiration every day in all I do.

Sherry Serafini:
I would like to thank my daughters Erika and Nikki for their love and support of an artform that sometimes takes over our lives! My dad and mom for their gifts of support and belief that anything is possible. And God, from whom all talents and gifts come.

Paulette Baron, Amy Katz, Sherry Serafini:
To the bead community, we present this book as a labor of love to all who treasure the art of beadweaving.